CLEP

Introductory Sociology Exam Secrets Study Guide

Dear Future Exam Success Story:

First of all, **THANK YOU** for purchasing Mometrix study materials!

Second, congratulations! You are one of the few determined test-takers who are committed to doing whatever it takes to excel on your exam. **You have come to the right place.** We developed these study materials with one goal in mind: to deliver you the information you need in a format that's concise and easy to use.

In addition to optimizing your guide for the content of the test, we've outlined our recommended steps for breaking down the preparation process into small, attainable goals so you can make sure you stay on track.

We've also analyzed the entire test-taking process, identifying the most common pitfalls and showing how you can overcome them and be ready for any curveball the test throws you.

Standardized testing is one of the biggest obstacles on your road to success, which only increases the importance of doing well in the high-pressure, high-stakes environment of test day. Your results on this test could have a significant impact on your future, and this guide provides the information and practical advice to help you achieve your full potential on test day.

Your success is our success

We would love to hear from you! If you would like to share the story of your exam success or if you have any questions or comments in regard to our products, please contact us at **800-673-8175** or **support@mometrix.com**.

Thanks again for your business and we wish you continued success!

Sincerely,
The Mometrix Test Preparation Team

Need more help? Check out our flashcards at: http://MometrixFlashcards.com/CLEP

TABLE OF CONTENTS

Introduction

Thank you for purchasing this resource! You have made the choice to prepare yourself for a test that could have a huge impact on your future, and this guide is designed to help you be fully ready for test day. Obviously, it's important to have a solid understanding of the test material, but you also need to be prepared for the unique environment and stressors of the test, so that you can perform to the best of your abilities.

For this purpose, the first section that appears in this guide is the **Secret Keys**. We've devoted countless hours to meticulously researching what works and what doesn't, and we've boiled down our findings to the five most impactful steps you can take to improve your performance on the test. We start at the beginning with study planning and move through the preparation process, all the way to the testing strategies that will help you get the most out of what you know when you're finally sitting in front of the test.

We recommend that you start preparing for your test as far in advance as possible. However, if you've bought this guide as a last-minute study resource and only have a few days before your test, we recommend that you skip over the first two Secret Keys since they address a long-term study plan.

If you struggle with **test anxiety**, we strongly encourage you to check out our recommendations for how you can overcome it. Test anxiety is a formidable foe, but it can be beaten, and we want to make sure you have the tools you need to defeat it.

1

Secret Key #1 – Plan Big, Study Small

There's a lot riding on your performance. If you want to ace this test, you're going to need to keep your skills sharp and the material fresh in your mind. You need a plan that lets you review everything you need to know while still fitting in your schedule. We'll break this strategy down into three categories.

Information Organization

Start with the information you already have: the official test outline. From this, you can make a complete list of all the concepts you need to cover before the test. Organize these concepts into groups that can be studied together, and create a list of any related vocabulary you need to learn so you can brush up on any difficult terms. You'll want to keep this vocabulary list handy once you actually start studying since you may need to add to it along the way.

Time Management

Once you have your set of study concepts, decide how to spread them out over the time you have left before the test. Break your study plan into small, clear goals so you have a manageable task for each day and know exactly what you're doing. Then just focus on one small step at a time. When you manage your time this way, you don't need to spend hours at a time studying. Studying a small block of content for a short period each day helps you retain information better and avoid stressing over how much you have left to do. You can relax knowing that you have a plan to cover everything in time. In order for this strategy to be effective though, you have to start studying early and stick to your schedule. Avoid the exhaustion and futility that comes from last-minute cramming!

Study Environment

The environment you study in has a big impact on your learning. Studying in a coffee shop, while probably more enjoyable, is not likely to be as fruitful as studying in a quiet room. It's important to keep distractions to a minimum. You're only planning to study for a short block of time, so make the most of it. Don't pause to check your phone or get up to find a snack. It's also important to **avoid multitasking**. Research has consistently shown that multitasking will make your studying dramatically less effective. Your study area should also be comfortable and well-lit so you don't have the distraction of straining your eyes or sitting on an uncomfortable chair.

 The time of day you study is also important. You want to be rested and alert. Don't wait until just before bedtime. Study when you'll be most likely to comprehend and remember. Even better, if you know what time of day your test will be, set that time aside for study. That way your brain will be used to working on that subject at that specific time and you'll have a better chance of recalling information.

Finally, it can be helpful to team up with others who are studying for the same test. Your actual studying should be done in as isolated an environment as possible, but the work of organizing the information and setting up the study plan can be divided up. In between study sessions, you can discuss with your teammates the concepts that you're all studying and quiz each other on the details. Just be sure that your teammates are as serious about the test as you are. If you find that your study time is being replaced with social time, you might need to find a new team.

2

Secret Key #2 – Make Your Studying Count

You're devoting a lot of time and effort to preparing for this test, so you want to be absolutely certain it will pay off. This means doing more than just reading the content and hoping you can remember it on test day. It's important to make every minute of study count. There are two main areas you can focus on to make your studying count.

Retention

It doesn't matter how much time you study if you can't remember the material. You need to make sure you are retaining the concepts. To check your retention of the information you're learning, try recalling it at later times with minimal prompting. Try carrying around flashcards and glance at one or two from time to time or ask a friend who's also studying for the test to quiz you.

To enhance your retention, look for ways to put the information into practice so that you can apply it rather than simply recalling it. If you're using the information in practical ways, it will be much easier to remember. Similarly, it helps to solidify a concept in your mind if you're not only reading it to yourself but also explaining it to someone else. Ask a friend to let you teach them about a concept you're a little shaky on (or speak aloud to an imaginary audience if necessary). As you try to summarize, define, give examples, and answer your friend's questions, you'll understand the concepts better and they will stay with you longer. Finally, step back for a big picture view and ask yourself how each piece of information fits with the whole subject. When you link the different concepts together and see them working together as a whole, it's easier to remember the individual components.

Finally, practice showing your work on any multi-step problems, even if you're just studying. Writing out each step you take to solve a problem will help solidify the process in your mind, and you'll be more likely to remember it during the test.

Modality

Modality simply refers to the means or method by which you study. Choosing a study modality that fits your own individual learning style is crucial. No two people learn best in exactly the same way, so it's important to know your strengths and use them to your advantage.

For example, if you learn best by visualization, focus on visualizing a concept in your mind and draw an image or a diagram. Try color-coding your notes, illustrating them, or creating symbols that will trigger your mind to recall a learned concept. If you learn best by hearing or discussing information, find a study partner who learns the same way or read aloud to yourself. Think about how to put the information in your own words. Imagine that you are giving a lecture on the topic and record yourself so you can listen to it later.

For any learning style, flashcards can be helpful. Organize the information so you can take advantage of spare moments to review. Underline key words or phrases. Use different colors for different categories. Mnemonic devices (such as creating a short list in which every item starts with the same letter) can also help with retention. Find what works best for you and use it to store the information in your mind most effectively and easily.

3

Secret Key #3 – Practice the Right Way

Your success on test day depends not only on how many hours you put into preparing, but also on whether you prepared the right way. It's good to check along the way to see if your studying is paying off. One of the most effective ways to do this is by taking practice tests to evaluate your progress. Practice tests are useful because they show exactly where you need to improve. Every time you take a practice test, pay special attention to these three groups of questions:

- The questions you got wrong
- The questions you had to guess on, even if you guessed right
- The questions you found difficult or slow to work through

This will show you exactly what your weak areas are, and where you need to devote more study time. Ask yourself why each of these questions gave you trouble. Was it because you didn't understand the material? Was it because you didn't remember the vocabulary? Do you need more repetitions on this type of question to build speed and confidence? Dig into those questions and figure out how you can strengthen your weak areas as you go back to review the material.

 Additionally, many practice tests have a section explaining the answer choices. It can be tempting to read the explanation and think that you now have a good understanding of the concept. However, an explanation likely only covers part of the question's broader context. Even if the explanation makes perfect sense, **go back and investigate** every concept related to the question until you're positive you have a thorough understanding.

As you go along, keep in mind that the practice test is just that: practice. Memorizing these questions and answers will not be very helpful on the actual test because it is unlikely to have any of the same exact questions. If you only know the right answers to the sample questions, you won't be prepared for the real thing. **Study the concepts** until you understand them fully, and then you'll be able to answer any question that shows up on the test.

It's important to wait on the practice tests until you're ready. If you take a test on your first day of study, you may be overwhelmed by the amount of material covered and how much you need to learn. Work up to it gradually.

On test day, you'll need to be prepared for answering questions, managing your time, and using the test-taking strategies you've learned. It's a lot to balance, like a mental marathon that will have a big impact on your future. Like training for a marathon, you'll need to start slowly and work your way up. When test day arrives, you'll be ready.

Start with the strategies you've read in the first two Secret Keys—plan your course and study in the way that works best for you. If you have time, consider using multiple study resources to get different approaches to the same concepts. It can be helpful to see difficult concepts from more than one angle. Then find a good source for practice tests. Many times, the test website will suggest potential study resources or provide sample tests.

Copyright © Mometrix Media. You have been licensed one copy of this document for personal use only. Any other reproduction or redistribution is strictly prohibited. All rights reserved.

Practice Test Strategy

If you're able to find at least three practice tests, we recommend this strategy:

Untimed and Open-Book Practice

Take the first test with no time constraints and with your notes and study guide handy. Take your time and focus on applying the strategies you've learned.

Timed and Open-Book Practice

Take the second practice test open-book as well, but set a timer and practice pacing yourself to finish in time.

Timed and Closed-Book Practice

Take any other practice tests as if it were test day. Set a timer and put away your study materials. Sit at a table or desk in a quiet room, imagine yourself at the testing center, and answer questions as quickly and accurately as possible.

Keep repeating timed and closed-book tests on a regular basis until you run out of practice tests or it's time for the actual test. Your mind will be ready for the schedule and stress of test day, and you'll be able to focus on recalling the material you've learned.

Secret Key #4 – Pace Yourself

Once you're fully prepared for the material on the test, your biggest challenge on test day will be managing your time. Just knowing that the clock is ticking can make you panic even if you have plenty of time left. Work on pacing yourself so you can build confidence against the time constraints of the exam. Pacing is a difficult skill to master, especially in a high-pressure environment, so **practice is vital**.

Set time expectations for your pace based on how much time is available. For example, if a section has 60 questions and the time limit is 30 minutes, you know you have to average 30 seconds or less per question in order to answer them all. Although 30 seconds is the hard limit, set 25 seconds per question as your goal, so you reserve extra time to spend on harder questions. When you budget extra time for the harder questions, you no longer have any reason to stress when those questions take longer to answer.

Don't let this time expectation distract you from working through the test at a calm, steady pace, but keep it in mind so you don't spend too much time on any one question. Recognize that taking extra time on one question you don't understand may keep you from answering two that you do understand later in the test. If your time limit for a question is up and you're still not sure of the answer, mark it and move on, and come back to it later if the time and the test format allow. If the testing format doesn't allow you to return to earlier questions, just make an educated guess; then put it out of your mind and move on.

On the easier questions, be careful not to rush. It may seem wise to hurry through them so you have more time for the challenging ones, but it's not worth missing one if you know the concept and just didn't take the time to read the question fully. Work efficiently but make sure you understand the question and have looked at all of the answer choices, since more than one may seem right at first.

Even if you're paying attention to the time, you may find yourself a little behind at some point. You should speed up to get back on track, but do so wisely. Don't panic; just take a few seconds less on each question until you're caught up. Don't guess without thinking, but do look through the answer choices and eliminate any you know are wrong. If you can get down to two choices, it is often worthwhile to guess from those. Once you've chosen an answer, move on and don't dwell on any that you skipped or had to hurry through. If a question was taking too long, chances are it was one of the harder ones, so you weren't as likely to get it right anyway.

On the other hand, if you find yourself getting ahead of schedule, it may be beneficial to slow down a little. The more quickly you work, the more likely you are to make a careless mistake that will affect your score. You've budgeted time for each question, so don't be afraid to spend that time. Practice an efficient but careful pace to get the most out of the time you have.

Copyright © Mometrix Media. You have been licensed one copy of this document for personal use only. Any other reproduction or redistribution is strictly prohibited. All rights reserved.

Secret Key #5 – Have a Plan for Guessing

When you're taking the test, you may find yourself stuck on a question. Some of the answer choices seem better than others, but you don't see the one answer choice that is obviously correct. What do you do?

The scenario described above is very common, yet most test takers have not effectively prepared for it. Developing and practicing a plan for guessing may be one of the single most effective uses of your time as you get ready for the exam.

In developing your plan for guessing, there are three questions to address:

- When should you start the guessing process?
- How should you narrow down the choices?
- Which answer should you choose?

When to Start the Guessing Process

Unless your plan for guessing is to select C every time (which, despite its merits, is not what we recommend), you need to leave yourself enough time to apply your answer elimination strategies. Since you have a limited amount of time for each question, that means that if you're going to give yourself the best shot at guessing correctly, you have to decide quickly whether or not you will guess.

Of course, the best-case scenario is that you don't have to guess at all, so first, see if you can answer the question based on your knowledge of the subject and basic reasoning skills. Focus on the key words in the question and try to jog your memory of related topics. Give yourself a chance to bring the knowledge to mind, but once you realize that you don't have (or you can't access) the knowledge you need to answer the question, it's time to start the guessing process.

It's almost always better to start the guessing process too early than too late. It only takes a few seconds to remember something and answer the question from knowledge. Carefully eliminating wrong answer choices takes longer. Plus, going through the process of eliminating answer choices can actually help jog your memory.

Summary: Start the guessing process as soon as you decide that you can't answer the question based on your knowledge.

7

How to Narrow Down the Choices

The next chapter in this book (**Test-Taking Strategies**) includes a wide range of strategies for how to approach questions and how to look for answer choices to eliminate. You will definitely want to read those carefully, practice them, and figure out which ones work best for you. Here though, we're going to address a mindset rather than a particular strategy.

Your odds of guessing an answer correctly depend on how many options you are choosing from.

Number of options left	5	4	3	2	1
Odds of guessing correctly	20%	25%	33%	50%	100%

You can see from this chart just how valuable it is to be able to eliminate incorrect answers and make an educated guess, but there are two things that many test takers do that cause them to miss out on the benefits of guessing:

- Accidentally eliminating the correct answer
- Selecting an answer based on an impression

We'll look at the first one here, and the second one in the next section.

To avoid accidentally eliminating the correct answer, we recommend a thought exercise called **the $5 challenge**. In this challenge, you only eliminate an answer choice from contention if you are willing to bet $5 on it being wrong. Why $5? Five dollars is a small but not insignificant amount of money. It's an amount you could afford to lose but wouldn't want to throw away. And while losing

$5 once might not hurt too much, doing it twenty times will set you back $100. In the same way, each small decision you make—eliminating a choice here, guessing on a question there—won't by itself impact your score very much, but when you put them all together, they can make a big difference. By holding each answer choice elimination decision to a higher standard, you can reduce the risk of accidentally eliminating the correct answer.

The $5 challenge can also be applied in a positive sense: If you are willing to bet $5 that an answer choice *is* correct, go ahead and mark it as correct.

Summary: Only eliminate an answer choice if you are willing to bet $5 that it is wrong.

8

Which Answer to Choose

You're taking the test. You've run into a hard question and decided you'll have to guess. You've eliminated all the answer choices you're willing to bet $5 on. Now you have to pick an answer. Why do we even need to talk about this? Why can't you just pick whichever one you feel like when the time comes?

The answer to these questions is that if you don't come into the test with a plan, you'll rely on your impression to select an answer choice, and if you do that, you risk falling into a trap. The test writers know that everyone who takes their test will be guessing on some of the questions, so they intentionally write wrong answer choices to seem plausible. You still have to pick an answer though, and if the wrong answer choices are designed to look right, how can you ever be sure that you're not falling for their trap? The best solution we've found to this dilemma is to take the decision out of your hands entirely. Here is the process we recommend:

Once you've eliminated any choices that you are confident (willing to bet $5) are wrong, select the first remaining choice as your answer.

Whether you choose to select the first remaining choice, the second, or the last, the important thing is that you use some preselected standard. Using this approach guarantees that you will not be enticed into selecting an answer choice that looks right, because you are not basing your decision on how the answer choices look.

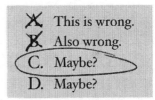

This is not meant to make you question your knowledge. Instead, it is to help you recognize the difference between your knowledge and your impressions. There's a huge difference between thinking an answer is right because of what you know, and thinking an answer is right because it looks or sounds like it should be right.

Summary: To ensure that your selection is appropriately random, make a predetermined selection from among all answer choices you have not eliminated.

Test-Taking Strategies

This section contains a list of test-taking strategies that you may find helpful as you work through the test. By taking what you know and applying logical thought, you can maximize your chances of answering any question correctly!

It is very important to realize that every question is different and every person is different: no single strategy will work on every question, and no single strategy will work for every person. That's why we've included all of them here, so you can try them out and determine which ones work best for different types of questions and which ones work best for you.

Question Strategies

⊘ Read Carefully

Read the question and the answer choices carefully. Don't miss the question because you misread the terms. You have plenty of time to read each question thoroughly and make sure you understand what is being asked. Yet a happy medium must be attained, so don't waste too much time. You must read carefully and efficiently.

⊘ Contextual Clues

Look for contextual clues. If the question includes a word you are not familiar with, look at the immediate context for some indication of what the word might mean. Contextual clues can often give you all the information you need to decipher the meaning of an unfamiliar word. Even if you can't determine the meaning, you may be able to narrow down the possibilities enough to make a solid guess at the answer to the question.

⊘ Prefixes

If you're having trouble with a word in the question or answer choices, try dissecting it. Take advantage of every clue that the word might include. Prefixes and suffixes can be a huge help. Usually, they allow you to determine a basic meaning. *Pre-* means before, *post-* means after, *pro-* is positive, *de-* is negative. From prefixes and suffixes, you can get an idea of the general meaning of the word and try to put it into context.

⊘ Hedge Words

Watch out for critical hedge words, such as *likely, may, can, sometimes, often, almost, mostly, usually, generally, rarely,* and *sometimes.* Question writers insert these hedge phrases to cover every possibility. Often an answer choice will be wrong simply because it leaves no room for exception. Be on guard for answer choices that have definitive words such as *exactly* and *always.*

⊘ Switchback Words

Stay alert for *switchbacks.* These are the words and phrases frequently used to alert you to shifts in thought. The most common switchback words are *but, although,* and *however.* Others include *nevertheless, on the other hand, even though, while, in spite of, despite,* and *regardless of.* Switchback words are important to catch because they can change the direction of the question or an answer choice.

⊘ Face Value

When in doubt, use common sense. Accept the situation in the problem at face value. Don't read too much into it. These problems will not require you to make wild assumptions. If you have to go beyond creativity and warp time or space in order to have an answer choice fit the question, then you should move on and consider the other answer choices. These are normal problems rooted in reality. The applicable relationship or explanation may not be readily apparent, but it is there for you to figure out. Use your common sense to interpret anything that isn't clear.

Answer Choice Strategies

⊘ Answer Selection

The most thorough way to pick an answer choice is to identify and eliminate wrong answers until only one is left, then confirm it is the correct answer. Sometimes an answer choice may immediately seem right, but be careful. The test writers will usually put more than one reasonable answer choice on each question, so take a second to read all of them and make sure that the other choices are not equally obvious. As long as you have time left, it is better to read every answer choice than to pick the first one that looks right without checking the others.

⊘ Answer Choice Families

An answer choice family consists of two (in rare cases, three) answer choices that are very similar in construction and cannot all be true at the same time. If you see two answer choices that are direct opposites or parallels, one of them is usually the correct answer. For instance, if one answer choice says that quantity x increases and another either says that quantity x decreases (opposite) or says that quantity y increases (parallel), then those answer choices would fall into the same family. An answer choice that doesn't match the construction of the answer choice family is more likely to be incorrect. Most questions will not have answer choice families, but when they do appear, you should be prepared to recognize them.

⊘ Eliminate Answers

Eliminate answer choices as soon as you realize they are wrong, but make sure you consider all possibilities. If you are eliminating answer choices and realize that the last one you are left with is also wrong, don't panic. Start over and consider each choice again. There may be something you missed the first time that you will realize on the second pass.

⊘ Avoid Fact Traps

Don't be distracted by an answer choice that is factually true but doesn't answer the question. You are looking for the choice that answers the question. Stay focused on what the question is asking for so you don't accidentally pick an answer that is true but incorrect. Always go back to the question and make sure the answer choice you've selected actually answers the question and is not merely a true statement.

⊘ Extreme Statements

In general, you should avoid answers that put forth extreme actions as standard practice or proclaim controversial ideas as established fact. An answer choice that states the "process should be used in certain situations, if..." is much more likely to be correct than one that states the "process should be discontinued completely." The first is a calm rational statement and doesn't even make a

11

definitive, uncompromising stance, using a hedge word *if* to provide wiggle room, whereas the second choice is far more extreme.

⊘ Benchmark

As you read through the answer choices and you come across one that seems to answer the question well, mentally select that answer choice. This is not your final answer, but it's the one that will help you evaluate the other answer choices. The one that you selected is your benchmark or standard for judging each of the other answer choices. Every other answer choice must be compared to your benchmark. That choice is correct until proven otherwise by another answer choice beating it. If you find a better answer, then that one becomes your new benchmark. Once you've decided that no other choice answers the question as well as your benchmark, you have your final answer.

⊘ Predict the Answer

Before you even start looking at the answer choices, it is often best to try to predict the answer. When you come up with the answer on your own, it is easier to avoid distractions and traps because you will know exactly what to look for. The right answer choice is unlikely to be word-for-word what you came up with, but it should be a close match. Even if you are confident that you have the right answer, you should still take the time to read each option before moving on.

General Strategies

⊘ Tough Questions

If you are stumped on a problem or it appears too hard or too difficult, don't waste time. Move on! Remember though, if you can quickly check for obviously incorrect answer choices, your chances of guessing correctly are greatly improved. Before you completely give up, at least try to knock out a couple of possible answers. Eliminate what you can and then guess at the remaining answer choices before moving on.

⊘ Check Your Work

Since you will probably not know every term listed and the answer to every question, it is important that you get credit for the ones that you do know. Don't miss any questions through careless mistakes. If at all possible, try to take a second to look back over your answer selection and make sure you've selected the correct answer choice and haven't made a costly careless mistake (such as marking an answer choice that you didn't mean to mark). This quick double check should more than pay for itself in caught mistakes for the time it costs.

⊘ Pace Yourself

It's easy to be overwhelmed when you're looking at a page full of questions; your mind is confused and full of random thoughts, and the clock is ticking down faster than you would like. Calm down and maintain the pace that you have set for yourself. Especially as you get down to the last few minutes of the test, don't let the small numbers on the clock make you panic. As long as you are on track by monitoring your pace, you are guaranteed to have time for each question.

⊘ Don't Rush

It is very easy to make errors when you are in a hurry. Maintaining a fast pace in answering questions is pointless if it makes you miss questions that you would have gotten right otherwise. Test writers like to include distracting information and wrong answers that seem right. Taking a little extra time to avoid careless mistakes can make all the difference in your test score. Find a pace that allows you to be confident in the answers that you select.

⊘ Keep Moving

Panicking will not help you pass the test, so do your best to stay calm and keep moving. Taking deep breaths and going through the answer elimination steps you practiced can help to break through a stress barrier and keep your pace.

Final Notes

The combination of a solid foundation of content knowledge and the confidence that comes from practicing your plan for applying that knowledge is the key to maximizing your performance on test day. As your foundation of content knowledge is built up and strengthened, you'll find that the strategies included in this chapter become more and more effective in helping you quickly sift through the distractions and traps of the test to isolate the correct answer.

Now that you're preparing to move forward into the test content chapters of this book, be sure to keep your goal in mind. As you read, think about how you will be able to apply this information on the test. If you've already seen sample questions for the test and you have an idea of the question format and style, try to come up with questions of your own that you can answer based on what you're reading. This will give you valuable practice applying your knowledge in the same ways you can expect to on test day.

Good luck and good studying!

Introduction to the CLEP Series

Your school requires you to take this CLEP Assessment in order to test the breadth and depth of your knowledge in a specified subject matter. Through CLEP Exams, you have the opportunity to earn credit or advanced standing at most of the nation's colleges and universities.

Because the issuance of your credit ensures competence in the subject area it is important that you take studying seriously and make sure you study thoroughly and completely.

Institutions, Social Patterns, and Social Processes

Molecular Anthropology

Molecular anthropology is a subdivision of physical anthropology that utilizes genetic analysis of DNA to determine evolutionary linkage. **DNA**, or deoxyribonucleic acid, is the substance that carries the genetic information of humans (and other organisms). DNA can be taken from fossils, for example, and compared to other ancient artifacts or the blood of living humans or other primates. Typically, molecular anthropologists look at relationships between antique and modern species, patterns of migration, or patterns of divergence. Much of this is accomplished by examining **haplogroups** or clusters of hereditary traits indicative of geographical origin.

Precedents for the Theory of Evolution

Charles Darwin's theory of evolution (discussed further elsewhere) was preceded by work and concepts of other researchers. In the 1700s, **Carolus Linnaeus** put together an extensive taxonomic classification of plants and animals, which was based on similarities and differences in physical attributes. Although he believed in creationism or divine creation of all things in the universe, Linnaeus' scheme provided a useful basis for later work and is still significant. Around the same time and into the 19th century, fossil records were being gathered that were counterintuitive to creationism as they showed discrepancies between these records and existing plants and animals. Darwin's father, **Erasmus**, was an evolutionist, writing a book called *Zoonomia* in 1794 in which he supported the shared ancestry of all animal species. Charles Darwin was also persuaded by the geologist **Sir Charles Lyell**, who put forth the concept of **uniformitarianism**, which said that natural forces operating then also explained past events and disputed the creationist theories of the age of earth.

Charles Darwin's Theory of Evolution

Charles Darwin set forth a theory of evolution or development from earlier forms or species. He coauthored a paper with Alfred Russel Wallace, who had similar views, in 1858 and published *On the Origin of the Species* in 1859. Much of Darwin's work was predicated by studying finches in the Galapagos. His theory is based on the process of **natural selection** or the preferential choosing of forms that have features that facilitate reproductive success. Organisms within a group vary, and those with characteristics that help them thrive and reproduce are more likely to pass on their characteristics. That is, they have an adaptive advantage. Evolution and natural selection illustrate the effect of environment on the genetic material that is more likely to be passed on to future generations, but they do not suggest that acquired characteristics are passed on.

Mendelian Genetics

Mendelian genetics is based on experiments performed by interbreeding of pea plants by **Gregor Mendel** in the 1850s. When Mendel crossed pure strains of pea plants with different characteristics, all F_1 or first generation plants had similar **phenotypes** or outward physical characteristics. However, when he did further breeding between different F_1 plants, the F_2 or second generation plants exhibited more than one phenotype. These observations led Mendel to postulate that there was a **dominant** form or trait that could conceal a **recessive** trait that was still present and could be passed on. The actual genetic makeup of an organism is its genotype, which we now know to be carried on chromosomes containing paired DNA (deoxyribonucleic acid) and made up of genes or basic hereditary units for various traits. **Alleles** are possible variants of genes.

If an organism has identical alleles, they are said to be **homozygous**, whereas if they have inherited two alleles that are slightly different, they are said to be **heterozygous** and will express the dominant allele.

Mendel's Views on Independent Assortment and Recombination

Gregor Mendel did additional work beyond that for which he originally postulated Mendelian genetics. He developed a **law of independent assortment** based on his observations that different traits were inherited separately from others. For example, inheritance of seed shape, coat color, type of pod, or stem length differences could show up independently during interbreeding and recombine in many ways. This **recombination** generates varieties that can provide the basis for natural selection. However, Mendelian genetics and his laws on independent assortment and recombination only provide a static situation and do not address evolution and change through genetic mutation.

DNA

DNA or **deoxyribonucleic acid** is the fundamental hereditary material of life and the basis of biochemical or molecular genetics. Structurally in humans and many other organisms, DNA is a double-stranded helix. Each DNA strand is made up of many molecules of the sugar **deoxyribose**, which is chemically bound to one of four bases, either **thymine** (T), **adenine** (A), **cytosine** (C) or **guanine** (G). One DNA strand is bound to the other in the helix through A-T or C-G interactions. DNA can duplicate itself by unwinding the strands and forming new complementary ones, making it crucial to the production of gametes (cells involved with sexual reproduction) and new cells. It is also used to encode for the manufacturing of proteins by serving as a template for **RNA** (ribonucleic acid). Three RNA molecules in sequence, a triplet, code for a particular amino acid used to produce proteins like enzymes, hormones and antibodies. Changes that occur in DNA molecules are known as **mutations**, which account for the majority of shifts through natural selection.

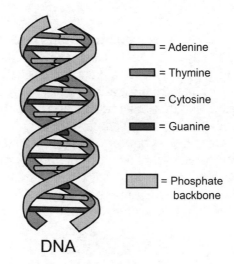

DNA

Cell Division

Usually cell division occurs through a process called **mitosis**, in which a cell divides into two daughter chromosomes with the same number of chromosomes as the parent cell. Mitosis occurs through life and mistakes such as different types of mutations can cause diseases such as malignancy. Sex cells or gametes undergo a slightly different course called **meiosis** in which a cell's nucleus divides into 4 nuclei each containing half the usual number of chromosomes. Each allele pair is broken up (called segregation by Mendel). When a male gamete or sperm fertilizes the female egg or ovum, a **zygote** is formed which grows rapidly into a child. Most cells have 23 pairs of chromosomes whereas a gamete has 23 individual ones. Fertilization can result in a variety of combinations accounting for the range in characteristics in progeny. Diversity can also result from an early event during meiosis called **crossing over**, which is the intertwining and subsequent swapping of some DNA on homologous chromosomes in gametes.

Genetic Mutations

Mutations in sex cells are hereditary; those in other somatic cells can cause disease. A **base substitution** or **single point mutation** is the substitution of one single base for another. If the mutation changes the amino acid that is encoded for, abnormal proteins associated with a disease state may be produced. **Chromosomal rearrangement** is a mutation in which part of a chromosome breaks and pieces are rearranged and reattached in a different configuration. It can transpire in a gamete, in the fertilized egg, or in other growing cells. Chromosomal rearrangement is primarily responsible for speciation, hereditary disorders, and malignancies.

Gene Pools and Genetic Evolution

The term gene pool is a collective expression for the entirety of genetic material in a breeding population or **deme**. A **gene pool** includes all alleles, genes, chromosomes and genotypes in that population. **Genetic evolution** refers to the shift in gene (in other words allele) frequency in a breeding population from one generation to the next. Most evolution results from the genetic transmission of variety through mutations which facilitate selective advantages. Other underlying forces that can play a role in genetic evolution include natural selection, random genetic drift, and gene flow.

Natural Selection

According to natural selection, individuals with **phenotypes** that thrive in a particular environment are selected over those with less favorable phenotypes or evident characteristics. Phenotypes can mask true genotype or genetic makeup if the organism possesses heterozygous alleles. Nevertheless, over time the features that are most adaptive or favored by natural selection will be preferentially selected. This means that there will be **directional selection** and eventual removal from the gene pool of recessive alleles that do not adapt well. Environmental changes can alter the directional selection and favor other phenotypes for certain traits. **Sexual selection** is a form of natural selection where organisms prefer to mate with a member of the opposite sex with a particular characteristic, such as feather color for birds or body shape for humans. There can also be a **balanced polymorphism**, in which two or more alleles for a trait tend to be passed on at relatively constant rate because each has equivalent advantages and disadvantages in a particular environment.

Random Genetic Drift

Random genetic drift is genetic change over generations that occurs coincidentally. Certain traits are passed on in a nonrandom fashion and eventually genotypic ratios change or traits are lost. The complete displacement of one trait over another is referred to as **fixation**, which can transpire more quickly in small populations. One type of **genetic drift** is **fission** in which a population splits for some reason to form new subpopulations. If there is an uneven split, a **founder effect** is said to occur. Genetic drift can also occur through **gamete sampling**. As genes are passed from one generation to the next, a large number of genetic combinations are possible during fertilization, which are unrelated to adaptation. Over generations, significant genetic drift can be observed in a population.

Random Gene Flow

Gene flow is the swapping of genetic material through breeding with other groups. Traditionally, populations in relatively close proximity often **interbreed**, and genes are passed along. The sequence of interbreeding can continue to other groups as well. At some point, gene flow may contribute to **natural selection** depending on the environment. Generally, gene flow can only occur within a species, which is a group of organisms that are genetically similar enough to create offspring that can survive and reproduce. Thus, gene flow can usually produce variety but not speciation or the development of new species.

Modern Synthesis Viewpoint on Evolution

The modern synthesis viewpoint on evolution integrates Darwin's theory of evolution with Mendelian genetics. It holds that new species can only occur when they are reproductively inaccessible to another. Genetic changes that transpire without resultant speciation are examples of **microevolution**. More momentous changes that occur over longer periods of time can produce speciation and are considered **macroevolution**. **Speciation** is the separation of a particular ancestral species into one or several successors. Both micro- and macroevolution occur via similar mechanisms such as mutations. The rate at which microevolutionary changes eventually lead to macroevolution is not usually consistent, as Darwin originally postulated. Contemporary models are built on the idea of **punctuated equilibrium**, or lengthy periods of stability interspersed with occasional evolutionary jumps. There are many possible explanations for punctuated equilibrium, such as extinction followed by invasion, substitution of a group with a highly adaptive trait, and the acceleration of certain transformations due to abrupt environmental changes.

Racial Classification for Human Diversity

Racial classification categorizes organisms supposedly based on some sort of common ancestry. **Phenotypical traits** believed to show shared genetic ancestry are selected as the basis of racial classification. For humans, early racial classification schemes were based on skin color. Today, an explanatory methodology concentrating on the understanding of certain differences is favored over racial classification schemes. This is because the so-called "races" are not biologically different. Traditional classifications identified three races as white, black, and yellow or Caucasoid, Negroid, and Mongoloid. However, skin colors vary widely, certain populations are not easily classified by these schemes, various combinations of features that might be considered important can occur, and phenotype is not always reflective of underlying genotype.

American Anthropological Association's *Statement on "Race"*

In 1998, the American Anthropological Association (AAA) issued a *Statement on "Race."* The statement says that there is more **variation** within so-called "racial" groups than between, and that historically all interacting groups have tended to **interbreed**. It further states that most diversity has occurred gradually and since physical traits are passed on independently of one another, racial classifications are **arbitrary** and **biased**. In addition, the AAA Statement declared that previously the notion of race was used mostly to impose and reinforce status differences. Eventually, the concept of "race" developed into a world view. It is the view of the AAA that all normal individuals have the ability to learn any cultural behavior and that any contemporary differences in performance between certain "racial" groups are the result of factors other than biological inheritance.

Factors That Determine Skin Color

There are many genes that affect **skin color**, although the exact number is unknown. Skin color is mainly determined by the relative amount of the chemical **melanin** in a person's epidermis or surface layer of skin. People with darker skins have more melanin, a natural sunscreen. Before the sixteenth century, most extremely dark-skinned persons occupied the tropics, a zone 23 degrees to either side of the equator. People living outside this tropical zone had lighter skin colors that gradually got lighter the further they were from the tropic zone. However, newer migratory patterns such as Asians moving to eventually produce Native Americans caused different skin color patterns. Historically, geographic differences in skin color were a result of natural selection, whereas later migration and today's technological advances lessened its significance in terms of skin color.

Advantages and Disadvantages of Dark Versus Light Skin Colors

People with a dark skin color have high levels of skin **melanin** which naturally screens out UV radiation, averts sunburn and consequently increases sweating as well as thermoregulation. **Thermoregulation** is the maintenance of a steady body temperature despite environmental changes. Individuals with dark skin color are less susceptible to diseases, skin cancer, and folate breakdown. **Folate** is an essential nutrient used in cell division and DNA assembly. Disadvantages of dark skin color are a reduced ultraviolet radiation absorption outside tropical areas which makes them more prone to bone diseases like rickets and osteoporosis because they cannot produce vitamin D from sunlight exposure. People with light skin color have no natural sunscreen, but the UV exposure does permit the body to produce vitamin D and lessen the possibility of rickets or osteoporosis. The negatives of light skin color are increased susceptibility to sunburn, disease, skin cancer, and folate destruction (leading possibly to neural tube defects in the fetus and diseases like spina bifida). Light skin color can impair spermatogenesis, depress sweating, and decrease thermoregulation.

Relationships Between Blood Groups, Adaptation, and Variation

The basis of blood grouping is the **ABO system**, which distinguishes people's red blood cells in terms of their **surface antigens**. There are 3 possible **alleles** (A, B or O), and combinations of these alleles give four possible **phenotypes** (A, B, AB, or O). A and B antigens trigger antibody production. These antigens are made up of protein and sugars. It has been demonstrated that individuals with certain ABO blood types are more susceptible to certain diseases. In particular, before smallpox was essentially eradicated in the 1970s, it was found that people with types A or AB blood were more prone to the disease, probably because the virus is antigenically similar to the A antigen. Therefore, A or AB individuals do not recognize it as foreign and do not make protective antibodies. The most prevalent group worldwide, type O individuals with neither an A nor B surface antigen, are apparently more prone to cholera, bubonic plague, and gastric ulcers.

Relationships Between Hemoglobin Subtypes and Disease

Hemoglobin is an iron-containing protein present in the red blood cells (RBCs) that transports oxygen. The normal **hemoglobin** allele is Hb^A, but there is another possible allele, Hb^S. People who are **homozygous** for the Hb^S allele have sickle-cell anemia characterized by crescent-shaped RBCs, inability to store oxygen, clogging of small blood vessels, and increased incidence of fatality. On the other hand, individuals who are **heterozygous**, Hb^A/Hb^S or sickle-cell trait, appear to be less

20

susceptible to malaria because malarial parasites cannot flourish in the abnormal hemoglobin yet the normal component wards off sickle-cell anemia. In areas where malaria is prevalent, the Hb^s is protective, making it in effect a genetic anti-malarial "drug." Other adaptations related to hemoglobin have been observed, such as Andeans who have developed the capacity to produce more hemoglobin and store more oxygen in response to the thin air in the region.

Influence of Natural Selection and Adaptation on Facial Features

Several facial features have been correlated with environmental differences. In particular, nose length has been statistically shown to follow **Thomson's nose rule**, which says that the average nose length increases in cold regions. This is an adaptive response because in a longer nose there are more membranes and blood vessels to moisten and warm the air as it is inhaled, making it advantageous in both dry and cold areas. Large average **tooth size** has been associated with populations such as Native Australians who traditionally were hunters and gatherers.

Influence of Natural Selection and Adaptation on Size and Body Build

Different body sizes have adaptive advantages in different climates. There is a tenet called **Bergmann's rule** which states that for two bodies of similar shape, the smaller one has more surface area per unit of weight and loses heat more. Therefore, **larger body sizes** which retain heat more effectively are more likely to be found in colder areas, and **smaller body sizes** are more prevalent in hotter regions. Observations on body shape tend to support **Allen's rule**, which asserts that body parts that stick out, such as limbs, digits, and ears, tend to be longer or larger in groups from warmer climates. The rationale is that this increases the surface area comparative to mass and allows for heat loss.

Reading of the Genetic Code of an Individual Cell

Cells consist of a **nucleus** containing chromosomes and the cytoplasm containing other structures serving other functions. **Chromosomes** are made up of a protein core with two strands of deoxyribonucleic acid (DNA) wrapped around them in a double helical formation bound through interactions between complementary bases, either A-T (adenine-thymine) or G-C (guanine-cytosine). During **replication**, the helix uncoils and the now unpaired bases pick up their complementary bases in solution. Thus when the cell divides during **mitosis**, there are two daughter cells with the same number of chromosomes. Partial unwinding of the helix allows for synthesis of proteins. Here, part of one strand of the DNA is used as a template for transcription by **messenger ribonucleic acid** (mRNA) which uses complementary bases, except that uracil (U) is substituted for thymine. The mRNA leaves the nucleus and travels to the ribosomes in the cytoplasm where transfer RNA (tRNA) reads the codes for production of amino acids and assembly of proteins. Each section of three nucleotides in DNA is a codon for a particular **amino acid**.

Human Genome

An organism's total genetic constitution is its **genome**. There was a **Human Genome Project** completed in 2003 that sequenced almost the complete human genome. Two different groups sequenced the genome of two different individuals. While work and analysis continues, 3.1 million base pairs were sequenced. It was found that the vast majority (as much as 98%) of DNA is **non-coding**, meaning it does not code for proteins. Functions of non-coding DNA include initiation and termination of coding sequences, regulation of gene function, and transport of other DNA. Coding sections are interspersed with non-coding ones. A **coding sequence** can code for multiple proteins depending on which portion is transcribed. There are RNAs with functions other than ciphering the

protein code, mostly as regulatory agents. It also appears that some DNA coding sequences are designed to produce these non-coding RNAs instead of proteins.

Equations Relevant to Genetics of Populations

For a particular allele assuming two forms (A and B):

- Calculate the **allele count**
  - Number of A alleles = (2 x no. of homozygous AA individuals) + no. of heterozygous individuals (AB)
  - Number of B alleles = (2 x no. of homozygous BB individuals) + no. of heterozygous individuals (AB)
  - Total allele count = no. of A alleles + no. of B alleles
- Calculate **frequency** of each allele
  - Frequency of A allele = no. of A alleles/total allele count = p
  - Frequency of B allele = no. B alleles/total allele count = q

Then the **Hardy-Weinberg equilibrium hypothesis**, which assumes the null hypothesis of no evolutionary change, is used to test the impact of evolution. From above, all genotypes should be the sum of the product of frequencies, thus in theory $p^2 + 2pq + q^2 = 1$. The null hypothesis can be tested by:

- Calculate expected frequency for each genotype by using p and q from above.
- Multiply each expected frequency by total number of individuals in population to get expected number for each.
- Compare expected and observed numbers for each genotype. If they do not concur, the null hypothesis is refuted.

Taxonomy of Primates

Taxonomy is a classification scheme for organisms that assigns them to certain categories or taxa based on their relationships and likenesses to other organisms. Many resemblances reflect their shared **phylogeny** or genetic relatedness. Organisms in the same category have **homologies** or traits that were inherited from the same ancestor. The levels of **zoological taxonomy** start with a kingdom at the top and go down through phylum, subphylum, class, infraclass, order, suborder, infraorder, super family, family, tribe, genus, species, and finally subspecies. Humans and other primates fit into the kingdom of Animalia or animals. The category of primates is at the order level, and it includes monkeys and apes in addition to humans. In fact, the field of primatology studies nonhuman primates including ancient and living apes, monkeys, and prosimians.

Human's Place in the Scheme of Primates

The term **primate** describes a member of a mammalian order with a large brain and complex hands and feet. There are two suborders, Prosimii or prosimians, and Anthropoidea or anthropoids. Prosimians are lower order nocturnal primates such as lemurs fitting into three infraorders and so on. Anthropoids are divided into two infraorders. One infraorder is Platyrrhini or platyrrhines with wide nostrils, notably New World monkeys. The other is Catarrhini or catarrhines, which includes Old World monkeys, apes, and humans. Categorically below that, catarrhines are separated into two super families of Cercopithecoidea, which includes Old World monkeys, and Hominoidea or hominids comprised of three families. These families are Hylobatidae with gibbons and siamangs, Pongidae represented by orangutans, and Hominidae or hominids, to which gorillas,

22

chimpanzees, and humans all belong. Modern humans are of the family Hominidae (hominids), tribe Hominini or hominins, genus Homo or human, species Homo sapiens (which also includes recent humans), and subspecies Homo sapiens sapiens.

Relationship Between Homologies, Analogies, and Convergent Evolution

The term **homology** refers to traits actually inherited from a common ancestor. **Analogies** are resemblances that have arisen through convergent evolution. In **convergent evolution**, analogous selective forces have acted on different organisms to generate similar adaptive traits. Thus, it appears that the two are closely related because of similar traits, but in fact they are not. Ideal taxonomic classifications rely only on homology, not analogy. Humans definitely fit into the same zoological family of hominid as previous humans, chimpanzees, gorillas, and other common predecessors.

Primate Tendencies of Anthropoids

Anthropoids are the suborder of the order primates to which humans as well as monkeys and apes belong. Early primates were arboreal tree dwellers, and thus all contemporary primates have characteristics reflecting this. Primates are distinguished by **five basic traits**. The first is the ability to grasp by having flexible five-digited hands and feet. Humans and some other primates also have opposable thumbs that can contact other fingers. Humans have lost this trait for their feet as they have adapted to upright, bipedal walking. Primates have a better sense of sight than smell. The primary tactile or touch organ in primates is the hand, mainly the fingerprint area. Primates have larger brains relative to body size and more brain matter devoted to cognition than other mammals. Most primates also have only one offspring, increasing prospects for developing learned conduct. Lastly, primates are generally very social.

Prosimians

Prosimians are the other suborder of primates besides anthropoids. Lemurs, lorises, and tarsiers fit into the Prosimii or prosimian suborder. The **prosimians** that have survived to the present day have done so primarily because they were active nocturnally and did not have to vie for survival with anthropoids that operated diurnally or mainly during the day. Today, the native habitat of prosimians is Madagascar for lemurs; Indonesia, Malaysia, and the Philippines for the tarsier; and Africa and Asia for lorises. Fossils show, however, that prosimians once lived in North American and Europe.

New World and Old World Monkeys

New World and Old World monkeys were reproductively inaccessible to the other. Both are anthropoids, but **New World monkeys** belong to the infraorder of platyrrhines characterized by a flat nose and often a prehensile or grasping tail. They are found in Central and South American forests. **Old World monkeys** belong to the infraorder of catarrhines which also includes apes and humans. All catarrhines have more pointed or sharp noses. Larger Old World monkeys like baboons and some macaques are generally terrestrial, whereas smaller examples tend to be arboreal and live in trees. The terrestrial species often show sexual dimorphism or trait differences between the sexes. All monkeys have arms and legs that are approximately of equal length, distinguishing them from apes and humans.

Characteristics of Apes

Apes and humans form the superfamily of **hominoids**, separate from the superfamily of Cercopithecoidea (Old World monkeys). Apes include the larger orangutans, gorillas, chimpanzees, and technically humans as well as the smaller gibbons and siamangs. The largest distinction between apes and other anthropoids is that they have **arms** that are longer than their legs. This enables them to swing under and across branches through trees using their hands, an ability called **brachiation**. Adults and larger apes that cannot brachiate safely due to weight have now adapted to terrestrial movement. Nevertheless, the way in which the shoulder and collarbone of both apes and humans are constructed indicates that all had a common brachiating predecessor.

Smaller Apes

The smaller apes include gibbons and siamangs, which are sometimes known as the "lesser apes." Both usually reside in **primary groups** with a bonded male, female, and preadolescent progeny. Gibbons are mainly arboreal and have lengthy arms and fingers facilitating brachiation as well as balance on the occasions they walk upright. They are very slim and nimble compared to other larger apes. A typical gibbon is only about a meter tall and weighs only 5 to 10 kilograms (up to 25 pounds). Their natural habitat is the forests of Southeast Asia. They eat fruits and sometimes insects or small animals.

Orangutans

Orangutans are considered "great apes" along with gorillas and chimpanzees. There are two extant species in the jungles of Asia that are part of the genus **Pongo** and the only representatives of the family Pongidae. Orangutans exhibit a high degree of sexual dimorphism, with the adult male much heavier than the female. The mature males are smaller than gorillas but larger than chimpanzees. Females and children are primarily arboreal whereas heavier males usually climb trees. They eat fruits, bark, leaves, and insects. Males tend to go out alone searching for food leaving the female and youngsters.

Gorillas

Gorillas are the most massive of apes. There are three extant subspecies of the species, which is technically called *Gorilla gorilla*. The native habitat of the smallest is various areas of Africa, the slightly bigger eastern lowland gorilla is found only in the Congo, and the biggest and rarest mountain gorillas are scattered. Just like orangutans, gorillas exhibit sexual dimorphism, with the male about twice as large as the adult female. Gorillas are for the most part terrestrial primates because although they have long arms reflecting their ancestry, they are too heavy to swing from trees. They eat a variety of primarily ground level vegetation. They are very social and tend to live in groups of up to 30 gorillas with one mature silverback gorilla as the lone breeding male.

Chimpanzees

Chimpanzees are the smallest of the so-called "great apes." There are two extant species, *Pan troglodytes* and *Pan paniscus,* which belong to the hominid family, genus **Pan**. A *Pan troglodyte* is the common chimpanzee, whose native habitat is various areas of Africa. They live primarily in tropical rain forests but are also found in woodlands or mixed regions. They eat mainly fruits but also small animals, eggs, and insects. The average adult female to male height is comparable to that in humans or .88 to 1. They are primarily arboreal, very social, and form a variety of social groups. The other representative species is *Pan paniscus,* the bonobo or pygmy chimpanzee. Bonobos are found only in the Democratic Republic of Congo in moist forests, and they have always been

24

arboreal. They are similar in size and female to male ratio as other chimpanzees. Their groupings are female-centric, and they have unusually frequent but often aggressive sex.

Behavioral Ecology and Fitness as Related to Primates

Behavioral ecology is the analysis of the evolutionary basis for social behaviors. It presumes the impact of natural selection, differential reproduction, and reproductive fitness. The concept of **fitness** means the ability to produce offspring that survive and reproduce. However, different social organizations in various primates illustrate diverse types of fitness. Some, like gibbons with strong male-female pair bonds, emphasize **individual fitness**, which is fitness quantified by the number of one's direct descendants. Others underscore **inclusive fitness**, the number of genes shared with relatives, evident in primates who defend the offspring of siblings.

Geological Time Scales

Geological times scales divide life as far back as that identified through fossil records. There are six eras and periods and epochs within all except the earliest eras. Fossils found in the same **stratum** or layer of earth are from the same time period or era. The oldest **Hadean era** began 4500 million years ago, the second oldest **Archaean era** started 3800 million years ago (m.y.a.), and the **Proterozoic era** (which had three periods) began 2500 m.y.a. Vertebrates, animals with backbones, were not observed until the **Paleozoic era** starting 544 m.y.a. and the only representative samples were fishes, amphibians, and early reptiles. The next **Mesozoic era** was when reptiles fully emerged, including dinosaurs as well as primitive birds. It began 245 m.y.a., had three periods (the Triassic, the Jurassic, and the Cretaceous), and ended with significant extinction of plant and animal life, including dinosaurs. The **Cenozoic or recent life period** (discussed on another card) began 65 m.y.a. Different plant life emerged during these periods as well.

Cenozoic Era

The Cenozoic era is the most recent. It began 65 million years ago with the **tertiary period**, which is divided into five epochs. The oldest epoch, the *Paleocene*, produced the mammals. Beginning 54 m.y.a., the *Eocene* epoch was a period of warm tropical climates in which the modern orders of mammals and anthropoids emerged and primates similar to prosimians were prevalent. About 38 m.y.a., the *Oligocene* epoch began, characterized by cooler, dry weather in the north, anthropoids in Africa, and growing distinctions between the primates. In the *Miocene* epoch, beginning 23 m.y.a., the cool, dry climate area extended toward middle latitudes, and Africa and Eurasia collided. The *Pliocene* epoch, which started 5 m.y.a., is characterized by emergence of Australopithecine hominids and Ardipithecus. The **quaternary period** of the Cenozoic era is divided into the Pleistocene and Holocene epochs. The *Pleistocene* or ice age epoch began somewhere around 1.6 to 1.8 m.y.a. and was a period of climatic changeability and glaciation and also the time that the genus Homo appeared. The modern or Holocene epoch began 10,000 to 11,000 years ago when warmer temperatures began and agriculture became prevalent.

Early Primates

Tropical and subtropical climates prevailed during the early **Cenozoic era** providing vegetation. **Early primates** were driven by adjustment to arboreal life and a heightened sense of sight. While there is equivocal evidence that some early primates probably existed during the Paleocene epoch, fossil records definitely confirm early primates during the next Eocene epoch (~54 to 38 m.y.a.). A 55-million-year-old skull of a euprimate, a mammal with some primate characteristics like frontward eyes and a large braincase, was recently found in China and named *Teilhardina asiatica*. A wide variety of prosimians lived in what we now call North America, Europe, Asia, and Africa,

25

which were all interconnected or almost connected (Africa). At some point, certain prosimians began to develop characteristics associated with anthropoids, such as more diurnal behavior and larger brains and eyes. By the Oligocene epoch (~38-23 m.y.a.), anthropoids predominated. There is fossil evidence primarily from Egypt of probable ancestors to New World monkeys, the parapithecid family, as well as the later catarrhines, the propliopithecid family which shares dentition patterns.

Miocene Epoch Hominoids

During the Miocene epoch (~23-5 m.y.a.), early **hominoids** antecedent to but different from present-day apes evolved. Fossils from the early part of the epoch indicate three species of the *Proconsul* group in Africa, characterized by dentition similar to current apes but a skeleton more like that of a monkey. Approximately 16 m.y.a. at the start of the middle part of the **Miocene epoch**, a **land bridge** developed between Eurasia and Africa providing migratory opportunities. Fossils of protoapes from this time have been discovered in various areas usually coexisting with our genus of *Homo erectus*. These include the extremely large *Gigantopithecus*, which probably lived in Asia until about 400,000 years ago. More recent finds from this time period include *Pierolapithecus catalaunicus*, from about 13 m.y.a. in Spain, which some believe is the last common ancestor to modern great apes including humans; *Sahelanthropus tchadensis* or Toumai, from about 7 to 6 m.y.a. in Chad, possibly the oldest known human descendant; *Orrorin tugenensis*, from about 6 m.y.a in Kenya, a bipedal creature with many resemblances to a chimp; and *Ardipithecus* (discussed elsewhere).

Bipedalism

Bipedalism, the ability to walk upright on two feet, is considered the fundamental feature that distinguishes early hominins from apes. The earliest identified and recognized ones belong to the genus *Ardipithecus,* examples of which have been found in Ethiopia dating from 5.8 to 4.4 m.y.a. Most experts believe that bipedalism developed during the Miocene epoch in some primates because of geological factors more than 5 million years ago. There was a shift toward a cooler, drier climate and more grassland in Africa. There was also a sinking of the Rift Valley and development of mountains in what is present-day Ethiopia, Kenya, and Tanzania. Primates east of this range started using bipedalism in order to navigate the grasslands more easily and view predators, while still sleeping and hiding in trees. Another explanation is that walking upright kept these hominins cooler due to less exposure to solar radiation. To the west of this range, the environment had more trees and was more humid, favoring chimpanzees.

Traits Other Than Bipedalism That Characterize Hominins

Hominins are the tribe that humans belong to. Early hominins had much smaller brains, similar in size to those of a chimpanzee, than modern humans. **Brain size** relative to other parts of the anatomy has increased over the ages because of the demands of upright bipedal locomotion. The **pelvic and trunk regions** need to be smaller for posture. Walking upright makes it difficult to have too large of a pelvic opening. Brain and **skull size** also became larger because humans have an extended period of childhood dependency. Early hominins had larger back teeth than modern humans because they needed them to chew tough, fibrous vegetation in the grasslands. As humans evolved, **dentition** has gotten smaller. Early hominins created and used **tools**, which was facilitated by bipedalism. Use of tools is still unique to hominins.

Early Hominins Ardipithecus and Kenyanthropus

Along with several of the *Australopithecus* species, these are two of the **earliest known hominins**, or human line after its division from ancestral chimps. Currently, *Ardipithecus kadabba* is considered to be the oldest known hominin because it appears to have been **bipedal**. Fossils dating from 5.8 m.y.a. were found in Ethiopia. Other members called *Ardipithecus ramidus* dating to 4.4 m.y.a. were also discovered in Ethiopia. *Kenyanthropus platyops* was discovered in Kenya and is considered by some to be a different branch of the human family tree because it has a flatter face and smaller molars. It dates to 3.5 million years ago.

Earliest Australopithecines

Australopithecines are prehistoric primates resembling humans dating to the **Pliocene epoch**. Six known species have been placed into this genus. The earliest example is *Australopithecus anamensis* found at two different sites in Kenya dating from 4.2 and 3.9 m.y.a. *A. anamensis* may have developed from *Ardipithecus ramidus*. It was bipedal and had thick molars and large canines. The species generally thought to be a predecessor to all later species of this genus was *Australopithecus afarensis* ("Lucy" and others) with fossil finds in Tanzania and Ethiopia dating it to between 3.8 and 3 million years ago. Fossils indicate many apelike attributes including dentition patterns, a cranial size only a little larger than that of a chimpanzee, and marked sexual dimorphism. Both of these Australopithecines were bipedal, however, which is the major reason they are considered human ancestors. There is another species called *A. garhi* discovered in Africa dating from 2.6 to 1.2 m.y.a.

Differences in Dentition Between Chimpanzees, Humans, and *A. Afarensis*

Early Australopithecines such as *A. Afarensis* are considered to be **dividing points** between chimpanzees and humans because although they were bipedal, they still had some qualities more reminiscent of chimps. In particular, the dentition pattern of *A. afarensis* is still closer to that of a chimpanzee than a human, reflecting their diet of coarse, fibrous savanna vegetation. Humans have much smaller back molars than the others, less pronounced canines, no diastema or gap between incisors and canines, and a more rounded, parabolic arch. Chimpanzees and *Australopithecus afarensis* both have relatively large molars, prominent canines, and diastemas, although the canine of the chimpanzee is much larger and more pointed. Adults of all three have a 2.1.2.3 dentition pattern in each quadrant of two/2 incisors, one/1 canine, two/2 premolars, and 3/three molars.

Evidence That Australopithecines were Bipedal

Australopithecines had a shorter and broader pelvis than apes, and the sacrum, which anchors the side bones, was wide. Their thigh bone was at an angle to the hip instead of straight as with an ape. They had a lumbar or lower spinal curve. Fossil records show that the foramen magnum or hole connecting the spinal cord to the brain was further forward and more centrally located in the Australopithecines than chimpanzees. All of these things make it easier to **walk upright**. The pelvises of Australopithecines are similar to but not exactly like those found in the later *Homo* species.

Gracile and Robust Australopithecines

Three species of more recent and relatively **robust** Australopithecines were found in Africa. Various theories suggest they developed from *A. afarensis* and that the **gracile** form either came first or overlapped in time with the robust forms. In any event, the smaller, less robust, so-called gracile species is represented by the South African *A. Africanus* which is dated to approximately 3 to

2 million years ago. Examples of **hyper-robust** Australopithecines include *A. robustus* and *A. boisei*; they had big, strong bones, teeth, and muscles and were thus very robust. They have been dated to ~2 to 1 m.y.a. and 2.6 to 1.2 m.y.a. and were found in South and East Africa, respectively. Their dentition was slightly different than earlier Australopithecines in that the canines were smaller, premolars were bicuspid, and molars were larger. The hyper-robust examples developed a sagittal crest at the pinnacle of the skull due to chewing. On average, all three weighed more and had larger brain sizes than earlier species

Division into the Two Genera of *Australopithecus* and *Homo*

It is believed that the hominins split into the **two genera** of *Australopithecus* and *Homo* more than 2 million years ago. The primary reason was reproductive remoteness. There was a time period where both existed in Africa until about 1.2 million years ago. The first known example of the *Homo* genus was *Homo habilis*, which had smaller teeth than Australopithecines and has been dated to approximately 2.4 to 1.4 m.y.a. *Homo erectus* lived around 1.9 to 1.4 million years ago. It had a bigger brain with regions that could regulate higher mental functions. The splitting of the genera has been explained in a number of ways. Some think that the two split from *Australopithecus afarensis* while others think only other Australopithecines evolved from it and eventually became extinct.

Possible Role of Tool Making

The oldest discovered tools are **Oldowan stone pebble tools**, which were found originally in Tanzania and later in other African areas. They date back as far as about 2.5 to 2 million years ago. There are two basic types: **cores**, used mainly for pounding, and **flakes**, utilized for cutting or scraping. Most experts have long believed that these tools were made by *Homo habilis*. However, there is some more recent evidence that at least one species of *Australopithecus*, *A. garhi*, also used stone tools around 2.5 million years ago in the area now called Ethiopia because these types of tools were found near the aforementioned fossils.

Homo Rudolfensis

Homo rudolfensis is a fossil discovered in Kenya, also known as **KNM-ER 1470**. It shows both a very large brain, indicative of *Homo* species, and also extremely big molars, suggestive of *Australopithecus* species. It has been variously dated to anywhere from 2.4 to 1.8 million years ago. The main reason it was assigned to the *Homo* genus was the large brain size. Some paleoanthropologists believe it is an example of *Homo habilis*, perhaps male, while others see differences between the two. The KNM-ER 1470 skull is larger than a typical *H. habilis* skull, does not have as striking a brow ridge, and has a longer and flatter face.

Relationship Between *Homo Habilis* and *Homo Erectus*

The Leakeys first discovered fossils of *Homo habilis* in Tanzania in 1960 and felt that it was a predecessor to *Homo erectus*. However, very recent fossil findings in Kenya suggest that the time frames for the two intersected and that sexual dimorphism existed in both. *Homo habilis* is now dated from 1.9 to 1.44 million years ago, and *Homo erectus* (earliest known called *H. ergaster*) is dated from 1.9 to 1 million years ago. Both species resided in close proximity for about a half million years. The *H. erectus* depended more on hunting and developed more specialized tools, however, and therefore show different dentition such as smaller back teeth.

Adaptive Traits of *Homo Erectus*

Homo erectus had a skeleton that was rough but surprisingly similar to modern humans, and they had longer legs than prior hominins. These traits facilitated **hunting**. They had a cranium about twice as large as the Australopithecines and close in size to *Homo sapiens*, but *H. erectus* had thicker skull bones, a wider and flatter shaped skull, and larger teeth, face, and jaws. All of these features were adaptations that facilitated hunting. They had learned about **fire** which made it possible for them to exist in caves, cook, and migrate to cooler climates. Fossils assigned to *Homo erectus* have been found as far from Africa as Dmanisi in Georgia (former Soviet Republic), Java, Italy, and several places in China. *Homo erectus* also made fairly complicated tools (discussed elsewhere). It cannot be proven whether or not they had a spoken language but the arrangement of their **vocal apparatus** was very similar to modern humans.

Pleistocene Epoch and the Evolution of Archaic Forms of *Homo Sapiens*

The Pleistocene epoch began about 1.8 million years ago. Towards the end of its **Lower period** around one million years ago, a number of ice ages or **glacials** interspersed with warmer periods called **interglacials**. During glacials, continental ice sheets pressed forward in North America and Europe and cooled the climate, and during interglacials they drew back. *Homo sapiens* lived during the latter part of the Middle and all of the Latter Pleistocene subdivisions. Early or archaic forms of *Homo sapiens* have been found in Europe, Africa, and Asia dating from about 300,000 to 28,000 years ago. They are separated into those who are believed to be ancestors of modern man and the Neanderthals. Teams have also discovered slightly earlier fossils that may be transitional (*H. heidelbergensis* in Germany) or a possible link between Neanderthals and anatomically modern humans (*H. antecessor* in Spain).

Neanderthals

The Neanderthals or *Homo sapiens neanderthalensis* are a group of archaic *H. sapiens* hunters. They primarily occupied Europe and the Middle East approximately 130,000 to 28,000 years ago, although examples have been found as distant as Siberia. **Neanderthal** fossils were discovered as long ago as 1856 in the **German Neander Valley**. Neanderthals display features that illustrate their adaptation to extremely cold glacial periods. They were relatively short and hefty with large trunks in comparison to their arms and legs. They had substantial nasal passages and long, wide noses. Their front teeth were massive, suggesting they may have used them for purposes other than just mastication, such as preparing hides to make clothing. Their facial features were wide and their brow ridges were sizeable. Later Neanderthal examples from the Wurm glacial time period starting around 75,000 years ago have less pronounced front teeth and brow ridges. This is presumably due to development of more sophisticated tools in the so-called **Mousterian tradition**. Neanderthals were the first hominids to bury their dead.

Relationship Between Neanderthals and Anatomically Modern Humans

It is currently held that Neanderthals were simply supplanted in Europe by **anatomically modern humans (AMHs)**. Experts feel that *Homo erectus* separated into two groups that evolved eventually into Neanderthals and AMHs. The average brain size of Neanderthals was smaller than AMHs, 1430 versus 1350 cubic centimeters. Most fossil records indicate differently shaped brain cases and other facial features. AMHs had more rounded and higher brain cases, a more prominent forehead, more distinct chins, less heavy brows, and less massive front teeth. It is felt that anatomically modern humans such as Cro-Magnon, Skhul, Qafzeh, and Herto began in Africa and

then migrated into Europe and Asia, displacing the Neanderthals and perhaps also interbreeding with them. Some call this the "out of Africa theory" or **Recent African Origin model**.

<u>DNA Evidence Supporting Differences</u>

A 1997 study comparing DNA from a Neanderthal's upper arm bone to that of a modern reference DNA sample indicated twenty-seven **discrepancies** as opposed to a maximum of eight **divergences** from different modern populations. More recent sequencing of nuclear and mitochondrial DNA (mtDNA) from another Neanderthal fossil indicates that the Neanderthal had a significantly dissimilar Y or male chromosome from modern humans, suggesting little procreation between the Neanderthals and anatomically modern humans (AMHs). An older study in 1987 examined mtDNA in women with ancestors from various areas. Mitochondrial DNA, which is extracted from the cytoplasm of cells, was selected because it is contributed only by the mother in the fertilized ovum. This investigation showed a great deal of variation in those of African descent. Using a technique called **molecular dating**, which assumes a certain mutation rate, it concluded that modern humans are descended from a woman living about 200,000 years ago ("Eve").

Theory of Multiregional Evolution

Multiregional evolution (MRE) is the theory that *Homo sapiens* evolved from *Homo erectus* in all areas occupied by humans. This is opposed to the **out of Africa theory**, which purports that the origin was only in Africa followed by movement to Europe and elsewhere (discussed further on other cards). The **multiregional evolution theory** was mainly put forth in the late 1990s by **Milford Wolpoff**, who contends that there has always been interbreeding and gene flow and that any type of selective improvement would be disseminated. He and his followers believe that the evolution from *H. erectus* to *H. sapiens* occurred regionally. This theory is supported by observations that distinctive regional features found today are evident in *Homo erectus* fossils found in the same area. According to multiregional evolution, if there was a common ancestor or "Eve," she existed far before the timeframe suggested by the out of Africa theory.

Homo Floresiensis

Homo floresiensis is a newly identified *Homo* species found on the Indonesian island of **Flores**. These fossils, dated from about 95,000 to as recently as 13,000 years ago, show miniature archaic humans derived from *Homo erectus*. They show extremely small skulls, approximately 370 cubic centimeters. It is believed that isolation on the island coupled with atypical evolutionary forces caused all animals there to exhibit either gigantism or dwarfism. *H. floresiensis* apparently made quite complex tools, used fire, and perhaps had some type of language. There was a volcano about 12,000 years ago in the region where these were discovered which obliterated them.

Disciplines That Often Work Together with Physical Anthropologists

Physical anthropologists often work in partnership with archeologists or other scientists. Whereas **physical anthropologists** glean information through looking at fossil records, **archeologists** examine artifacts. Complementary disciplines include **paleontology**, the examination of ancient life through fossil records, and **palynology**, the analysis of ancient plants and ecosystems utilizing pollen samples. For example, plant crystals or phytoliths are often found on teeth or artifacts. Other types of scientists that may work in conjunction with physical anthropologists and archeologists are geologists, geographers, physicists, and chemists. The relatively new and high-tech procedure of **remote sensing** is increasingly being employed. Remote sensing is the utilization of satellite imaging and aerial photography to detect potentially valuable ground sites.

Use of Bone Biology in Physical Anthropology

Bone or **skeletal biology** is the examination of bone as a biological tissue. It is fundamental to the work of **physical anthropologists**. Bone can be studied from many different perspectives, such as its genetics, biomechanics, osteology, or paleopathology. **Biomechanics** refers to the way in which movement is constructed, osteology is the examination of skeletal differences and their causes, and paleopathology looks at the way in which disease or injury affected skeletal remains. **Forensic anthropology** generally uses bone biology to look at more recent human remains in order to figure out a cause of death and other characteristics. An overall term for body measurement research is **anthropometry**.

Stratigraphy and Relative Dating of Remains

Fossils, artifacts, and other material remains can be dated either by relative or absolute (chronometric) dating. **Relative dating** is facilitated by **stratigraphy**, the examination of how the earth sediments into discrete layers or strata. The **law of superposition** states that unless a disturbance has occurred, new layers are superimposed over older ones and stratigraphy can be used to establish a relative chronological sequence. Relative dating ascertains a time frame for a particular remain based on the strata it is found in and relative to remains of other plants and animals that presumably lived at the same time. It does not give a definitive date. Older remains are found in deeper strata and vice versa. Relative dating also uses fluorine absorption analysis, which utilizes the principle that bones from the same period take in similar percentages of fluorine.

Radiocarbon Dating for Absolute Dating of Remains

Absolute dating of remains is more precise dating through more scientific techniques than relative dating. Each radiometric technique quantifies **radioactive decay**. Organic materials up to 40,000 years old are dated using ^{14}C, the radioactive isotope of carbon (stable version ^{12}C) which is absorbed in plants from cosmic radiation and later in animals that eat these plants or other animals. The time of death or vestiges from a fire can be dated using the carbon-14 half-life of 5730 years, when half of the isotope is converted into stable nitrogen (^{14}N). Small samples can now be dated using **accelerator mass spectrometry (AMS)** which actually counts the number of carbon-14 atoms.

Non-Carbon-Based Radiometric Dating Techniques for Absolute Dating of Remains

Very old materials from a half-million years ago or more can be dated by looking at the conversion of the much longer half-life radioisotope of **potassium ^{40}K** into the gas **argon-40** (potassium/ argon or K/Ar dating). This method is used to date inorganic rocks and minerals (primarily volcanic rock) by heating the rock to allow the release of trapped argon gas. A more accurate modification of this technique is argon/argon or Ar/Ar dating which calculates the decay of one argon isotope into another (^{40}Ar to ^{39}Ar). **Uranium series dating** uses fission tracks from decay of the uranium isotope ^{238}U into lead, ^{234}U into thorium, or other uranium isotopes to date materials anywhere from 1000 to 1 million years old. Similar time periods for rocks and minerals can also be established using **thermoluminescence**, which quantifies the energy captured from radioactive decay in nearby soil, or **electron spin resonance (ESR)**, which measures the accumulation of electrons on crystalline materials.

Dendrochronology for Absolute Dating of Remains

Dendrochronology or **tree-ring dating** is used for absolute dating of wood or charcoal materials up to about 11,000 years old. Tree growth is indicated by a new ring every year. Climatic variations affect the ring pattern, which should be similar in all area trees from the same time period. For example, wide rings indicate wetter years, while narrow ones point to dry years. Ring patterns on trees can be crossdated or matched by observation and statistical analysis, and this crossdating can also be used to pinpoint dates for wood or charcoal samples from ancient buildings or other artifacts. The technique can only be used with tree species that thrive in climates with distinct seasons such as juniper, oak, and pine.

Methods of Dating Remains Beyond Stratigraphy and Absolute Dating Techniques

Any dating method based on comparing cultural shifts is considered a **cultural technique**. One legitimate example is **seriation** or the recognition that there is a regular substitution of one artifact style for another. **Paleomagnetism**, which can only be used to date materials with magnetic minerals from about the last 2000 years, is another technique based on the movement of the earth's magnetic poles and their documented positions. **Obsidian hydration** is a method that can be used to date volcanic glass up to 800,000 years old. It is founded on the principle that obsidian glass forms a hydration layer over time as it reacts with water. Bones can be dated utilizing **amino acid racemization** or a shift in polarity of aspartic acid.

Culture and Enculturation

Culture is the totality of knowledge, beliefs, customs, practices, and social behaviors embraced by man as a member of society. A society is a structured community bound by shared factors. **Enculturation** is the process by which culture is discovered and passed on through generations. Humans are unique in that they are capable of learning culture consciously and unconsciously. Children are taught specific cultural attitudes, but they also undergo enculturation unconsciously through observation of behavior. Anthropologists hold that all human populations have equal capacities for developing a culture and that anyone can learn any cultural customs under the right conditions.

Role of Symbols in Enculturation

A symbol is something that *represents* something else. Use of **symbols** and symbolic thought is the uniquely human capacity that permits us to learn **culture**. A symbol can be verbal or nonverbal. Most human symbols are related to a language used by a particular culture. No other animal has developed a communication system anywhere near as complex as the languages of humans. Human cultures also use nonverbal symbols that are representations of other things, such as a flag for a country or religious practices with other implications. Humans are distinctively capable of storing, sorting out, and using information.

General Aspects of Culture

The most basic attributes of culture are that it is **learned** and **symbolic** (both discussed elsewhere). In addition, culture is shared or conveyed within a society. Each culture operates from a set of core or basic **central values**. These values assimilate the culture essentially into a patterned system. As certain values evolve, other parts of the system also change. Cultural behavior can be adaptive in response to particular circumstances. Culture is also all-inclusive, meaning all aspects of cultural life are included, not just those that may be considered refined or educated. Culture includes things like the way in which a particular society deals with natural urges, the extent to which they embrace modern science and inventions, or what they choose to advertise in the media.

Cultural Similarities and Differences Between Chimpanzees and Humans

Chimpanzees share many cultural similarities with humans. They (and other primates) can learn and adapt their behaviors, but their capacity for cultural learning is not as fully developed as humans. Chimpanzees make tools out of stones and other materials, albeit more primitive ones than humans. Tool manufacture and use by chimpanzees is only occasional as opposed to habitual for humans. Chimpanzees also hunt, but humans use tools for hunting and employ it as a basic survival strategy. Sharing of food and cooperation is innate to humans, whereas chimpanzees only occasionally practice sharing or cooperation. Some of the biggest differences are related to mating and kinship ties. Most human cultures generally practice exogamy, marriage outside their own social group, as well as marriage outside their own biological group. Their pair bonds usually are more exclusive than those of chimpanzees. Chimps mate temporarily at the time of female estrus. Humans mate at any time of year. Kinship ties are broken after adolescence in chimps, whereas humans continue to retain those ties.

Theories for the Dawn of Behavioral Modernity by Anatomically Modern Humans

Various theories place the advent of behavioral modernity by anatomically modern humans (**AMHs**) anywhere from 45,000 to 165,000 or more years ago. **Behavioral modernity** signifies the use of symbolic thought and cultural creativity to behave like modern humans. Richard Klein and others adhere to the theory that the dawn of human creativity occurred abruptly in Europe about 45,000 years ago subsequent to early mutations in Africa that reprogrammed the human brain for greater capacity for language and communication. It is impossible to prove this theory, but several pieces of archaeological evidence dispute it. Sophisticated tools made over a wide range of time in Africa suggest the human creativity may have originally occurred there and that it was probably a gradual learning process. Most African finds of complicated tools predate Klein's approximation, going back as far as 164,000 years ago in South Africa and possibly further in other areas. It is clear that creative expression had extended to the Middle East by 43,000 years ago with findings such as shell and bead jewelry from that time period.

Universal, General, and Particular Traits of Cultures

All human cultures have universal, general, and particular **patterns of culture**. **Universal traits** shared by all *Homo sapiens* cultures include: lengthy infant dependency; a complex brain with capacity for use of symbols, tools, and language; continuous (not cyclical) sexuality; food sharing; and some sort of family structure. All human cultures have an incest taboo, or ban on marriage or mating between those they consider close relatives, usually resulting in exogamy. **Generalities** are cultural characteristics that occur in some but not all societies. For example, the nuclear family is considered to be the ideal kinship group in some cultures and not in others. **Particularity** refers to a cultural trait or pattern that is unique to a culture. Modern transportation and interaction between cultures have made particularity increasingly rare. Nevertheless, cultures usually incorporate traits to their own needs in different ways. For example, life events like marriage and death are universals but they are practiced differently among various cultures.

Possible Levels of Culture

Cultural traditions can be practiced on a national, international, or sub-cultural basis. For example, certain foods are consumed primarily in one country, all over the world, or within a specific subculture. A **national culture** encompasses those beliefs, behaviors, values, and organizations shared by people of one specific nation. **International culture** refers to traditions that stretch beyond national borders through diffusion and learning, such as Catholicism. Within nations,

33

subcultures that practice unique cultural traditions can exist. Subcultures usually derive from differences in ethnicity, language, religious convictions, class, or regionalization.

Ethnocentrism, Cultural Relativism, and Human Rights

Ethnocentrism is the formation of an opinion about another cultural based on one's own cultural standards. Implicit in **ethnocentrism** is the conviction that our culture is superior to another. Thus, from an ethnocentric point of view, unfamiliar practices in other cultures may be deemed improper or abnormal. This point of view is particularly controversial at present because Western cultures tend to view practices such as female genital mutilation in some African and Middle Eastern countries or child labor in other regions as violations of **human rights**. The United Nations has enumerated internationally recognized human rights in several documents. **Cultural relativism** is the somewhat conflicting stance that behaviors should be judged only within the framework of the culture where they occur, not based on external standards.

Cultural and Indigenous Intellectual Property Rights

Cultural rights are those privileges that certain groups such as indigenous societies and religious and ethnic minorities are entitled to retain. **Cultural rights** include use of an indigenous language or traditional practices. **Indigenous intellectual property rights (IPR)** is a somewhat similar concept. Intellectual property rights are designed to preserve the basic beliefs and principles of an indigenous culture by allowing them to retain control over their unique knowledge base and applications. For example, traditional medicines, domesticated food, dances, and rituals would all be covered under IPR. Much of the push for intellectual property rights has been based on the potential for commercialism and outside economic gain.

Mechanisms of Cultural Change

Cultural change often occurs through **diffusion** or the exchange and borrowing of cultural attributes between societies. This diffusion can occur directly through business dealings, intermarriage, or conflicts. It can also transpire indirectly through a series of intermediaries or through force and subjugation. When two cultures are in steady contact, change can occur via **enculturation** or the exchange of cultural features. Another means of cultural change is **independent invention** or **ingenious problem solving** by people when faced with challenges. The modern world is faced with rapidly changing cultural changes as globalization, the increasing interdependence of nations, brings many cultures in contact through media, high-tech forms of communication, business dealings, migration, and travel.

Real Versus Ideal Culture

Ideal culture refers to what people profess is the proper behavior and what they say they actually do. Cultural attitudes are put forth collectively and publicly, but individuals also think and interpret these cultural values and ideas. **Real culture** is the way in which people actually behave as monitored by an anthropologist. Real and ideal culture do not necessarily equate to one another. In addition, individuals often break certain rules of convention. These breaks with **ideal culture** can range from simple violations like driving too fast to much more serious ones like murder.

Mometrix

Typical Ethnographic Field Techniques

Ethnographers typically employ one or more of the following field techniques:

- Direct observation of behavior including participating in community life during the study, possibly keeping a diary and field notes
- Conversation with and interviewing of the people; may use a formalized interview schedule
- Use of the genealogical method which uses diagrams and symbols to chronicle kinship relationships
- Working with local consultants or experts
- Gathering of life histories of certain individuals through thorough interviewing
- Discovery of local beliefs and perceptions (discussed further elsewhere)
- Longitudinal or long-term research involving recurring visits
- Team research involving many ethnographers
- Research designed to address a particular problem

Emic and Etic Approaches and World Views

Emic and etic approaches are different ways of looking at the beliefs and perceptions of a culture and categorizing them. Ethnographers who utilize an **emic approach** try to understand the native's point of view by relying on local cultural informants to enlighten them about what is important in the culture. The **etic method** is a more external approach. Here, the scientifically-trained ethnographer uses observation to categorize behavior. Anthropologists using an etic approach must be as objective as possible. Some combine both approaches in field work. **World views** can also be emic or etic, meaning they categorize things from the perspective of the involved culture or from a scientific viewpoint respectively.

Survey Research

Survey research is the examination of a sample group of a society and then making inferences about the society as a whole through statistical analysis. In **survey research**, the **sample** is a small but representative group of individuals or respondents. There are many ways of selecting the sample group, including questionnaires or solicitation. The best type of group is a random sample in which all people in the population have an equal probability of selection. Survey research uses **impersonal data collection**. Generally, responses for variables or attributes that can be categorized (for example, age group, gender, or income level) are collected. Survey research is often used in conjunction with ethnography, particularly when analyzing more complex, heavily-populated societies.

Nonhuman Primate Forms of Communication

Other nonhuman primates cannot speak, but they do use **call systems**. They have a restricted number of sounds or calls that they can generate when confronted with environmental stimuli. They can control the intensity and length of time of the call, but nonhuman primates can utter only one call at a time. Call systems are generally species specific. Various researchers have shown that nonhuman primates, particularly chimpanzees, can be taught or actually share skills that are innate to language. They (Washoe, Lucy, etc.) have been taught American Sign Language (ASL) by humans. The chimps have in turn transmitted it to offspring and other chimps. **Cultural transmission** through education is an elemental attribute of language. Apes have also shown capacities for two other linguistic essentials: **productivity** or the ability to create new intelligible expressions, and **displacement** or the capability of describing things or occurrences that are not in the present.

Language

Language is a system of communication. Humans utilize both spoken and written **language**, distinguishing them from other primates. Language uses words as symbols to represent the things for which they stand. It is constantly undergoing change. Language is transferred culturally, different communities have unique languages, and humans have capacities for linguistic productivity and displacement (discussed elsewhere). Recent studies have identified a gene called **FOXP2** that is apparently associated with the origin of language. A British family (KE) was found to have some members with the same genetic FOXP2 sequence as chimpanzees in conjunction with a speech defect in which they could not execute fine enough lip and tongue movements for intelligible speech. Other KE family members without this speech deficit had a different FOXP2 sequence. This implies that a mutation in this gene offered primates who had it a selective linguistic and cultural advantage. DNA analysis on a variety of samples indicates that this mutation occurred about 150,000 years ago.

Kinesics and Forms of Nonverbal Communication

Language refers to spoken and written communication, but communication between humans can also be **nonverbal**. **Kinesics** is the investigation of communication through nonverbal forms such as body movements, facial expressions, the way in which a person stands, or the gestures they use. **Cultural differences** are reflected in the way people use nonverbal communication, for example how closely they stand to the other person or the use of gestures like bowing. The same gesture can have a different meaning in another culture. Our **moods** are often reflected in how we use nonverbal communication (our stance, for example) as well as how we vary our verbal communication through changes in the tone of our voice.

Descriptive Linguistics

Descriptive linguistics is the scientific analysis of a spoken language. It can be divided into four components or areas of study. **Phonology** is the analysis of a particular language's speech sounds including its phonemics, distinguishing speech sounds, and its phonetics, the way in which these sounds are produced. Distinguishing speech sounds or phonemes are not the same in all languages. **Morphology** is the linguistic study of word formation or the way in which sounds are put together to create morphemes, the smallest meaningful unit of speech (or writing). The totality of morphemes and their meanings in a language is its **vocabulary** or lexicon. The last component of descriptive linguistics is **syntax**, the layout and order of words into phrases and sentences.

Phonemes

Phonemes, which are the minimum sound contrasts that differentiate meaning in a given language, are indicated by a slash on either side. For example, in English /r/ and /l/ indicate that r and l are **phonemes**. If the sound is not distinctive in a given language, it would be enclosed in brackets instead. There can be minute phonetic differences in the manner in which a particular phoneme is pronounced under different circumstances, such as how it is paired with other sounds. These differences may be expressed phonetically within brackets with some sort of different connotation or symbol. For example, vowel sounds fit into this category because the same vowel is often pronounced differently depending on the word construction. Differences in vowel sounds are produced by varying the height of the tongue and its relative front to back position.

Focal Vocabulary

A focal vocabulary is a set of specific terms and classifications unique to a certain group or culture. A **focal vocabulary** pertains to the focus of activity or experience of that group. It could be unique to a particular society as a whole, for example cultures that have multiple, differentiating terms for things they come in contact with often. It could also encompass terms for insiders to a particular activity within a larger culture, for example unique terms that sports fans use. Other members of the culture generally are not privy to these terms.

Fields Involved with Meaning in Language

The overall term for the study of a language's meaning system is **semantics**. Semantics looks at the interrelationships between words, phrases, and sentences. The term can also refer to the analysis of symbols or the study of logic. **Ethnosemantics** refers to the study of vocabulary classifications and the distinctions within them. Ethnosemantics covers the domains or groupings of associated things or concepts in each language such as kinship ties, terms for colors, aspects of disease (ethnomedicine), the taxonomy of plant life (ethnobotany), and descriptions of the universe (ethnoastronomy).

Sociolinguistics

Sociolinguistics is the study of language within a social and cultural context. People utilize the same language in different ways depending on factors like gender, class, ethnic background, and power. Individuals vary their speech or practice style shifts in different social situations, particularly ordinary conversation as opposed to more formal contexts. **Dialects** coexist within Standard English (SE) in the United States, and there are similar situations in other countries. Some languages have high and low dialects, called **diglossia**. Sociolinguists have observed that in general, women tend to use more polite terms than men. Multiple negation use is greater in men than women and is inversely related to class position. Most languages have honorifics or terms of respect that are used. Language differences that still get the point across are all valid according to the principle of linguistic relativity, but there is often social stratification and evaluation based on the way in which people use their language and what is considered fashionable.

Black English Vernacular

Black English Vernacular (**BEV**) is the term used for a dialect spoken in the United States by some urban black youths, in rural areas, and often casually by others as well. The phonology and syntax used in BEV resembles southern dialects. Some linguists feel that the dialect has African roots but the exact development of BEV is unclear. One difference between BEV and **Standard English (SE)** is that r's are often dropped between vowels. Another is the omission in Black English Vernacular of forms of the verb *to be* in the present tense and often *-ed* in the past tense. BEV speakers generally do not add an *-s* to distinguish plurality either.

Historical Linguistics

Historical linguistics is the analysis of languages over time. Practitioners construct family trees of languages. The base or trunk of the tree is the **protolanguage** or the original language which is ancestral to a number of modern daughter languages. Closely linked languages are separated into **linguistic subgroups**. More than 6000 years ago, there was a protolanguage termed **Proto-Indo-European (PIE)** from which Romance, Germanic, Celtic, Indic, and other language subgroups all developed. The Romance languages of Spanish, French, Italian, and Romanian all developed from Latin. Two branches of Germanic languages arose from a prototype: Western Germanic including languages like Dutch and English, and Northern Germanic including languages like Swedish and Danish. Language development was dependent on factors like immigration, trade, and conquest, and similar languages do not always reflect similarities in culture.

Terms and Ideas Associated with the Arts

The arts, also known as forms of **expressive culture**, include any mode that creates something beautiful or thought-provoking. Therefore, the arts are wide-ranging and include literature, visual arts like painting, music, dance, and drama. Any expressive form that awakens an aesthetic reaction can be considered a piece of art. **Aesthetics** are the qualities or ideas of what is artistic. Art need not be beautiful if it evokes an emotional response. What is considered a complete piece of art is subjective and biased in terms of community standards. To any extent, a person's cultural background influences what they consider to be aesthetically pleasing. Modern day art forms extend to things like film and other media, large installation pieces, and performance art.

Role of the Individual in Producing Art in Different Cultures

Generally, in Western societies, art works are likely to be creations of an **individual** working alone and identified as the artist. The artist tends to create the entire piece, although there are exceptions such as Rodin who only created the original mold for his sculptures. In non-Western cultures, production of art is often a **collective** venture and individual artists may not be recognized. By and large, artists in these cultures are more open to changing a design or allowing others to work on the project. Some art forms such as music and drama are inherently collective ventures. Certain societies make it possible for artists to be well-paid specialists, whereas art may be more individualistic in non-subsidized situations.

Ethnomusicology

Ethnomusicology combines the disciplines of music and anthropology. It compares types of music around the globe and looks at them within the context of culture and society. Ethnomusicologists generally do fieldwork. They often look at the origins of music, the social aspects of it, its biological roots, the role of folk music forms, and the traditions associated with singing or other musical forms. Music apparently began early in human history; the earliest known instrument is a 43,000 year old bone flute found in Slovenia. A number of experts have suggested a selective advantage for early humans who used music, primarily because of its social aspects.

Relationship Between Media Exposure and Culture

Media, which encompasses many forms of mass communication, plays a substantial role in contemporary culture. It reaches even small towns in remote places. Individuals exposed to **media** process, decipher, and assign meaning to its text relative to their **cultural experience**. They place value on and select different media for a variety of reasons that suit them. These reasons include things like validation, education, indulging fantasies, and curiosity. Television is a particularly powerful form of media. Various studies have documented the correlation between television content and cultural behavior.

Sports and Media in Different Cultures

Sports coverage in the media is pervasive around the world. Yet different **sports** are favored in different countries, certain nations do better internationally in particular Olympic sports, and there is differentiation in performance in team versus individual sports from athletes of different nations. One reason is the coverage and commentary that **media** in different countries provide for specific sports. Another is the emphasis placed on **winning** in a particular culture and the way in which this emphasis is expressed in the media. Cultures that are work- and achievement-oriented such as the United States tend to produce greater individual athletes and grant more latitude when they do not win. Cultures where one's identity is defined by status or family, such as Brazil, are less likely to generate winning athletes and overlook failure.

Social Stratification

Terms Related to Gender

Gender is the sex of an individual. Biologically, **gender** is determined by chromosomal makeup, with women having two X chromosomes and men having an X and the distinguishing Y chromosome. Males and females have different primary and secondary sexual characteristics. On average, the two genders exhibit sexual dimorphism or differences in traits such as weight, strength, or length of life. Many gender differences are culturally determined. Traditionally, cultures tended to assign gender roles or responsibilities and activities that they felt were appropriate to one sex or the other. An associated concept is the assignment of **gender stereotypes**, prevalent but oversimplified attitudes about gender characteristics. **Gender stratification** is the disparate distribution of social capital (for example, power, prestige, or independence) between the sexes.

Division of Labor by Gender Patterns

Various societies as a whole generally have activities that are performed by males, others that are carried out by females, and some that are **swing activities**, meaning either gender may do them. Typical **male activities** include things like hunting large animals, working in stone, boatbuilding, and fishing. Typical **female activities** include cooking, gathering firewood and vegetables, doing laundry, and spinning. Tasks that either sex might do include planting crops, harvesting, milking, preserving, and making pottery. Although the exact task may differ, the amount of time spent related to subsistence is roughly the same for males and females in most societies. Domestic work, however, is largely a female domain. One study showed that in the majority of societies, males do virtually no domestic work and even if they do, the females still do the bulk of it.

Common Gender Differences in Child Care and Sexual Standards

In about two-thirds of societies, **females** have more authority over the care, management, and discipline of **young children**. This is largely related to the fact that women tend to form a closer bond early with the child (through breastfeeding, for example) and are more invested in the child's survival as their reproductive capacity is more limited than the male's. However, there are societies in which males have more authority or it is shared. **Sexual standards** are different between the sexes. About seventy five percent of studied societies allow more than one spouse for a man, but multiple spouses for a woman are almost nonexistent. A double standard with regard to greater restrictions on premarital sex for women is held in over forty percent of cultures, and a similar percentage of societies place greater restrictions on females about extramarital sex.

Gender Roles and Stratification in Foraging Societies

Foraging societies have differences in the activities typically performed by men and women, but they generally have **less gender stratification** than food-producing cultures. Female activities are limited by frequent pregnancy, periods of lactation, and caring for children. Thus they tend to do the **gathering** while the men usually do the **hunting and fishing**. Foraging societies are generally more egalitarian and less stratified in many ways including gender roles and dominance than food-producers or more modern cultures. This is because there is less of a domestic-public dichotomy in these cultures. There is less opportunity to separate the domestic and public spheres, the latter of which generally represents more prestige in other types of cultures.

Gender Roles and Stratification in Horticultural Societies

Horticulture is a simplified form of agriculture in which small plots of land are worked without the help of animals or irrigation systems. Both matrilineal and matrilineal-descent structures, traced through women or men respectively, are found depending on the society. The cultures also define the residency after marriage as either matrilocality or patrilocality, meaning the couple lives in either the mother or father's community. In **matrilineal, matrilocal societies** such as the Iroquois (tribes originally from the New York area), the women controlled the local economy and living arrangements. **Matrifocal societies** in general have less social stratification than **patrilocal ones**. In societies where women have political power (matriarchy), the power differential is less than in patriarchies. **Patrilineal-patrilocal societies** tend to have increased gender stratification largely as a result of exposure of the men to public arenas such as warfare and trade. Patriarchal societies tend to have more violence, even in today's world.

Gender Roles and Stratification in Agricultural Societies

In about half of horticultural societies, women are the main **cultivators**, whereas more **complex agricultural cultivation** is generally done by men. Agriculture is more labor-intensive and requires more strength. **Agricultural societies** tend to elevate the role of men because of the development of beliefs that extra-domestic work outside the home is more valuable. Women in agricultural societies tend to have more children and spend more time in the home. They may contribute to subsistence activities but these may still be done within the home. Lineage, residency patterns, and sexual standards often shifted as societies became agricultural. Agricultural societies tend to be less rigid about descent groups, they are less likely to practice polygyny (more than one wife), and female sexuality is usually restricted more.

Relationship Between Industrialization and Gender Roles and Stratification

The spread of industrialization in the early twentieth century played a big role in differentiation between gender roles. Prior to that, women and men both worked as wage laborers. As mass production techniques created the need for fewer laborers, the perception grew that women were unsuitable for factory work and should remain at home. These **gender role perceptions** were always present during the twentieth century during cycles of high unemployment, and they waned when women were needed, such as during wartime. Paid employment for females has been on the rise since World War II, initially in traditionally female jobs like nursing or teaching but now in a range of positions. Over the years, the percentage of women (including married ones) working has steadily increased while the percentage of working men has decreased. On average, women still make less than men for the same job but the **wage gap** is closing. The majority of contemporary jobs do not require hard physical labor, which also contributes to less stratification.

Sexual Orientation

An individual can have a primary sexual attraction to the opposite sex, the same sex, or both sexes, known as **heterosexuality**, **homosexuality**, and **bisexuality**, respectively. There is actually a fourth orientation called **asexuality** or lack of interest in or attraction to both sexes. Many contemporary Americans view sexual orientation as having a biological basis. The relative contribution of biology to sexual orientation is currently unknown, but it is certain that sexual norms are partially shaped by culture. There are cultures with traditions that inherently change individual sexual patterns over time. Some societies engage in male-male sexual activity for specific reasons, and also practice heterosexuality when it is needed for reproduction. Sexual practices as well as the revealing of them is highly-dependent on how a particular culture views them, which can change over time.

Nuclear and Extended Families

A nuclear family is a kin group generally made up of parents and children living together in the same home. From an anthropologist's point of view, there are two types of **nuclear family**: one's family of orientation into which they were born and raised, or the one created through marriage and birth of children. The nuclear family is the major unit in many but not all societies. Some societies are arranged in extended family households where a couple and all their unmarried children as well as married sons and their wives and children all live and play various roles in the same household. **Collateral households** are extended families comprised of siblings and their families. Extended and collateral households are more prevalent among the poor. There are other societies that have relatively informal mating rituals and living arrangements, some that recognize more than one official father, and some that practice unconventional family organizations such as polygamy.

Changes in Kinship and Household Organization Patterns in US over Last Forty Years

Over the last forty years, the percentage of **family households** (married couples with or without children plus other household arrangements) has declined, while **nonfamily living arrangements** have increased. Today, over a quarter of the American population lives alone or in some other unconventional configuration, and the traditional nuclear family comprises only about 23% of households. Factors contributing to these changes include increased mobilization, economic independence of women, and a divorce rate that has hovered around 50% for the last three decades. The average size of families and households has decreased slightly over a similar time period in both the United States and Canada. North Americans are increasingly isolated from attachments to their extended kinship group and more dependent on other friendships or their immediate family (spouse and children). These changes do not necessarily apply in countries and cultures with different priorities.

Descent Group Affiliations

Traditionally, descent group affiliations have been **unilineal**, meaning they use only one line, either matrilineal or patrilineal, to define descent. Descent groups have an **apical** or original ancestor from which members descend. If the descent pattern can be demonstrated by identification of the ancestors, it is a **lineage**. If the descent pattern cannot be directed traced but is merely stipulated, it is called a **clan**. Many descent groups can identify a lineage back a number of generations and a clan before that. It is easier to maintain lineages and clans if people maintain local residence. Some people do not associate themselves strictly with matrilineal or patrilineal descent, instead choosing and practicing a more flexible rule called **ambilineal descent**.

Kinship Calculation

Kinship calculation, the way in which individuals in a particular society determine kinship, is culturally dependent. People **calculate kinship** through their own ego or unique egocentric perspective. A **genealogical kin type** reflects the actual hereditary relationship, whereas a **kin term** (for example "aunt") may not reflect actual hereditary relationships and can be used to indicate social relationships. In North America where the primary kinship group is the nuclear family, kinship ties are generally calculated **bilaterally**. This means that these ties are generally viewed in the same way through both males and females. In other words, your mother's brother and your father's brother are both considered your uncle.

Kinship Symbols and Genealogical Notations

On a genealogical chart, the **individual** or **ego** is indicated by a gray square regardless of sex. The symbol for a male is a triangle and a circle for a female. Sometimes the sex of the ego is given by using a gray triangle or circle. An equal sign (=) between a male and female indicates marriage; if there is a slash through the sign (⌷), that means the two are divorced. A vertical line (⌷) indicates the person or people are descended from another, and sibling relationships are shown by two vertical lines connected to a horizontal one. **Kin notations** are letters that serve to describe the relationship to the ego. They are husband (H), wife (W), father (F), mother (M), son (S), daughter (D), brother (B), sister (Z), and C for child.

Lineal Kinship Terminology

Americans value the nuclear family and generally use **lineal kinship terminology** in calculating kinship. The basic attribute of the lineal system is that it discriminates between lineal and collateral relatives. Using the individual or ego as the point of reference, a **lineal relative** is any person antecedent to or descending from the ego on the direct line of descent. Lineal relatives are generations of parents and children. Other kin such as siblings, their children, aunts and uncles, and cousins are all **collateral relatives**. Relatives through marriage are considered **affinals**. Each triangle (male), circle (female), or square (ego) is assigned a color based on whether they are lineal, collateral, or affinal. Relationships that are considered equivalent may be given the same number, such as 1 for mother, 2 for father, 3 for any uncle (FB or MB), and 4 for any aunt (FZ or MZ). Lineal kinship terminology is used in industrialized nations and foraging societies. There are three other types of kinship terminology used in other types of societies: bifurcate merging, generational, and bifurcate collateral terminologies.

Bifurcate Merging Kinship Terminology

Bifurcate merging kinship terminology is generally used with unilineal (matrilineal or patrilineal) descent groups and gender-oriented postmarital residence rules. It is prevalent in societies that are economically dependent on horticulture, agriculture, or raising livestock. In a **bifurcate merging system**, the individual ego separates their mother's side from their father's and sees same-sex siblings of the dominant parent as the same relative. Therefore, in a patrilineal culture, one's father and his brother are equivalent (F=FB=kin group 2), and in a matrilineal society, a person's mother and her sister are viewed similarly (M=MZ=kin group 1). In both cultures, the opposite sex parental sibling (MB or FZ) is viewed as being in a different group (3 or 4).

Generational Kinship Terminology

Generational kinship terminology consolidates together all male or female members of the same parental generation. Therefore, the terms used for a generation do not distinguish between sides of the family. This type of terminology is used with flexible, ambilineal types of associations and rules for residence. It is prevalent in economies that are horticultural, agricultural, or foraging in nature. Individuals in societies that use this type of terminology tend to regard their aunts and uncles closely, similar to their actual parent. On a chart, all females in the preceding generation are indicated by a "1" enclosed in a circle and all males are shown as a "2" within a triangle.

Bifurcate Collateral Kinship Terminology

Bifurcate collateral kinship terminology uses specific terms for each person in the parental generation. It also assigns a different kin term or number to each one. There are six classifications that someone from the parental group could fall into: mother (M or 1), father (F or 2), mother's brother (MB or 3), mother's sister (MZ or 6), father's brother (FB or 5), or father's sister (FZ or 4). The ego may call each parent's siblings by different names, perhaps reflective of the different cultural backgrounds of each. The situations in which kinship is viewed through this type of terminology are very diverse.

Parallel and Cross Cousins

Exogamy is the custom of marrying outside one's own group. Most societies practice some form of exogamy, and adhere at least in principle to a taboo against incest. **Incest** is defined as forbidden sexual relations with someone considered to be a near relative. A close relative is classified differently in various cultures. **Parallel cousins** are children of two same sex siblings, two brothers or two sisters. **Cross cousins** are children of different sex siblings. In an industrialized country like the United States, sexual conduct between either parallel or cross cousins as defined above is considered taboo. However, in matrilineal or patrilineal societies, an individual identifies with their mother or father's side of the family. Therefore, in these cultures, parallel cousins are anyone of the same generation and descent group as the ego and sexual conduct with them is taboo. Anyone belonging to the non-dominant side of the family is technically a cross cousin but is not considered a relative; therefore, sexual contact is not considered taboo and in fact is often encouraged.

Theories About the Taboo Associated with Incest

Incest is taboo in most societies, although it does occur. Ancient Egypt, for example, had a high percentage of documented sibling marriages for several centuries. There are many theories as to why there is a taboo associated with sexual relationships with close relatives, but most do not fully explain it. Some believe that the revulsion to incest is instinctive. Others suggest that incestuous interbreeding produced biological degeneration. Some feel early taboos developed to direct sexual feelings outside and therefore preserve the family structure. Others have proposed that familiarity breeds contempt, which is somewhat born out in situations where non-relatives have grown up together. Another explanation is that exogamy was practiced early on as an adaptive mechanism to guarantee alliances and mix genetic material. More contemporary work suggests that much of the taboo associated with incest is really cultural, not biological.

Endogamy and Homogamy

Endogamy is mating or marrying someone from the same clan or kinship group to which one belongs. The term can be extended to other definitions of group such as religious affiliation or ethnicity. The Indian caste system that was practiced until about sixty years ago is an extreme example of **endogamy** (discussed further elsewhere). Another example is royal endogamy, which has been practiced in various forms in a number of societies as a means of consolidating power or retaining the sacredness associated with royalty. Royal endogamy has sanctioned brother-sister marriage (for example, earlier Hawaiians and Polynesians) and cousin marriage (for example, cousin marriage in a number of European monarchies). **Homogamy** means intermarriage between members of the same social class or socioeconomic group. Homogamy is often practiced in contemporary society.

Indian Caste System

The Indian caste system, which was legally outlawed in 1949, was a form of forced **endogamy**. It stratified people into permanent groups according to birthright. There were five classes or **varna**. Within each varna in a particular area of India there were subcastes or **jati** that were also ranked. Intermarriage was only allowed between people in the same jati. Within a specific neighborhood, castes were often defined by occupation. People belonging to the lowest or untouchable varna

44

were considered impure, and others were put off by even casual dealings with the untouchables. Sexual contact with someone of a lower caste was highly discouraged, particularly between a higher caste woman and a lower caste man. Marriage between different descent groups was common, however. Although outlawed, remnants of the caste system remain today.

Traditional Marriage

Traditionally, marriage is defined as a joining together of a man and a woman in which children born to the woman are accepted as the legitimate offspring of the two. The anthropologist Edmund Leach identified **six rights** that accompany marriage in most cultures. The first is inherent in the above definition, which is establishment of the legal father of a woman's offspring, regardless of whether or not the male is the true biological father. Marriage generally gives one or both partners a monopoly on the other's sexuality, privileges to the labor of the other, and rights to the other's property. Usually it creates shared property for the benefit of the children. Additionally, marriage sets up a socially recognized relationship of kinship by marriage to the other's relatives. **Conjugal** means relating to marriage such as conjugal rights, and **natal** refers to something relating to birth such as the natal family.

Same-Sex Marriage Rituals in Certain Cultures and Contemporary Society

There are some cultures that recognize forms of **same-sex marriage** for social or practical purposes. In the Sudan, it is acceptable for two Nuer women to marry if the father of one of them has no male heirs. The woman whose father has no male heirs acts as the pater or socially recognized father to continue the kinship line, but men are chosen to have sex with and impregnate the "wife" in the pair. Various Native American groups had arrangements where individuals of the same sex were paired and assumed roles of the other gender for practical purposes. Today, we think of same-sex couplings in terms of homosexual pairings, and the union called marriage is unavailable to most. Some countries such as Canada have passed legislation to secure full marriage rights to same-sex pairs, and a few states in the United States allow legal unions with most of the benefits of marriage.

Bridewealth and Dowry

In certain societies, particularly nonindustrial ones, marriage is viewed not only as a union between two people but also as an **alliance** between groups. Bridewealth and dowry are vestiges of this viewpoint. **Bridewealth** or progeny price refers to marital gifts given to a wife and her kin by the husband's group. Conversely, **dowry** refers to considerable gifts bestowed to the husband's family by the wife's group. In societies (mainly patrilineal) that practice bridewealth exchange, it is used to pay back the wife's family for loss of her services and companionship and to legitimize the progeny. Dowry, which is also a product of patrilineal type cultures and a lower status for females, has been practiced mostly in India. In cultures that practice dowry, the women are seen as additional responsibilities being transferred to the husband. Obligatory dowry was proscribed in India in 1961 but the tradition continues to an extent.

Sororate and Levirate

There are two forms of maintenance of marital alliances when a spouse dies. **Sororate** refers to the practice in which a widower marries the sister of his late wife or, if she had no sister, another women from her group. By doing so, the man can keep his bridewealth and maintain group alliances. Both patrilineal and matrilineal cultures are known to practice sororate. **Levirate** is the practice in which a widow marries the brother of her late husband. It was an ancient Jewish custom

and is practiced in many African cultures today. The purpose again is to continue established alliances. Often, the widow and her new husband do not actually live together.

Patterns of Divorce

Divorce, the official dissolution of a marriage, is more likely to occur in societies where women have more power. This power could be attained through the increased status and lineage of a traditional **matrilineal** (and usually matrilocal) society. For example, in the matrilineal society of Hopi of the Oraibi pueblo, the divorce rate was extremely high. In modern-day Western societies, the divorce rate is also relatively high, particularly in the United States. Since 1960, the divorce rate in the United States has approximately doubled. Factors contributing to this pattern include gainful employment of many women, the perceived need for romantic love within marriage, stress, the importance placed on independence, and the relative lack of religious affiliation. The economic situation of the individuals plays a big role, as divorce is less prevalent during bad economic times or in homes where the woman is not gainfully employed.

Monogamy and Polygamy

Monogamy is the practice of marriage or maintaining a sexual relationship with only one person at a time. In contemporary Western societies, **serial monogamy** is common due to divorce and other opportunities. **Polygamy** or plural marriage, the custom of having more than one spouse at a time, is uncommon in Western society. There are two possible forms of polygamy: **polygyny**, in which the man has more than one wife, and **polyandry**, in which the woman has more than one husband. Polygyny is more widespread than polyandry. Polygyny is not necessarily practiced by all men in cultures where it is promoted, however. Reasons for polygyny include more household output, perceived status, and childbearing. In many of these arrangements, the first wife has the most power, including decision-making regarding subsequent spouses. The practice of polyandry is much more infrequent, usually in situations where a male might be away from home a great deal. Most polyandrous societies are in southern Asia.

Cultural Evolution

Evolutionism is perhaps the earliest theoretical perspective preoccupying anthropologists starting in the late nineteenth century. L. H. Morgan's 1877 treatise *Ancient Society* supported the concept of **unilineal evolutionism**, which supposes that all cultures travel through a series of stages in their development. He defined these stages in order as **savagery**, **barbarism**, and **civilization**. The stages of savagery and barbarism each have three distinct phases that cultures go through before reaching civilization. Criticisms of Morgan's view are that some very complex societies developed without proceeding through all these stages. Another early proponent of evolutionism was E. B. Tylor who utilized unilateral evolutionism in 1889 to suggest a similar progression related to religion. He said religion evolved through cultural stages of animism, polytheism, monotheism, and ultimately science. Evolutionists believe that different cultures use independent invention to arrive at similar final goals.

Boasians

F. Boas first proposed the concept of **four-field anthropology** using a historical, rather than evolutionary, approach to anthropology. In 1940, he published a book called *Race, Language, and Culture*. Boas and his followers expounded upon the idea of **historical particularism**, which asserts that different cultural histories are not comparable and that dissimilar paths can still result in similar cultural results. The **Boasians** essentially rejected the validity of cross-cultural comparison, a technique which is still used today. They also emphasized the importance of diffusion between cultures in addition to the possibility of independent invention. Most subsequent theoretical perspectives do not favor an individualistic approach.

Functionalism

The theoretical perspective of **functionalism** originated in Great Britain in the mid-20th century. It focuses on the way in which sociocultural practices operate in contemporary society. There are two schools of thought that could be considered functionalism. The first was espoused by **B. Malinowski** in his 1944 treatise *A Scientific Theory of Culture, and Other Essays* and elsewhere. He said that all customs and institutions in a culture are interrelated, and that the development of customs is based on satisfaction of universal biological needs. **A. R. Radcliffe-Brown** saw functionalism slightly differently. He emphasized that societies should only be studied in their present configuration as anything else was simply conjectural. He and others also stressed the importance of structural functionalism, the concept that all cultural systems have a structure and that practices within them maintain that structure. An extension of these ideas is **Panglossian functionalism** which advocates that deviations from the norm can impair the scheme.

Configurationalism

Configurationalism regards culture as integrated and patterned. The most well-known proponent of **configurationalism** was **Margaret Mead**. Her landmark book *Coming of Age in Samoa* from 1928 compared female adolescent sexual behavior in Samoa and the United States. It and later works support the idea that culture was more important than biology or race in determining human behavior and personality. In her studies, Mead illustrated the unique patterns and configurations of societies without regards to history. Another anthropologist who embraced configurationalism was **Ruth Benedict**.

Neo-Evolutionism

Neo-evolutionism is a theoretical viewpoint first presented in the 1950s in response to other perspectives that ignored the relationship between evolution and culture. **Neo-evolutionism** had two main proponents at that time. Both felt that specific cultures can evolve through different pathways and that there are primary causes for cultural progression. The first promoter was **Leslie White** who wrote *The Evolution of Culture.* He espoused general evolution, the development of culture evident in anthropological records, and felt that the greatest measure of advancement is the amount of energy captured. The other was **Julian Steward** who wrote *Theory of Culture Change*. Steward was one of the first investigators exploring cultural ecology or ecological anthropology, which looks at the connections between cultures and environmental factors. He believed that technology and the environment were the greatest causes of cultural progression. **Multilinear cultural evolution** is an ideology shared by most modern anthropologists.

Cultural Materialism

The main advocate of cultural materialism was **Marvin Harris**. The core philosophy behind **cultural materialism** is that the **societal infrastructure** is the most important aspect, and that this infrastructure determines the structure and superstructure of the culture. The infrastructure is comprised of systems that are vital for existence such as economics, technology, production, and procreation. Social, familial, allotment and consumption patterns form the structure of the society. The final cultural stratum of superstructure includes elements that are least important to survival such as religion, philosophy or recreation.

Cultural Determinism

Determinism is the belief that everything is caused by some other force or determinant. **Cultural determinism** views anthropology as a science that finds determinants or causes that produce certain effects. Thus, many anthropologists who adhere to other basic theoretical perspectives are also cultural determinists because they incorporate scientific methods. Influential anthropologists who incorporated cultural determinism include Margaret Mead (who felt culture was a major determinant), Marvin Harris (who wrote several books about science and culture), and the neo-evolutionist Leslie White. The latter two felt that infrastructure was a major determinant.

Structuralism

Structuralism is a theoretical perspective connected primarily with **Claude Levi-Strauss**. **Structuralism** sets forth the theory that all human minds have a number of common characteristics that lead people in different cultures to think in the same way. These **universal mental characteristics** include things that encourage classification and imposition of structure, such as the necessity to impose order on various relationships and the tendency to see things in binary opposition instead of in a continuum. In other words, humans in all cultures tend to see differences as distinct categories rather than disparities of degree.

Anthropological Theories That View Culture as More Influential Than the Individual

The neo-evolutionist **Leslie White** thought that individuals were insignificant relative to the cultural forces; he also believed that so-called "great" men were simply creations of timely cultural forces. He coined the term *culturology* for cultural anthropology. Another scholar called **Alfred Kroeber** also emphasized the command of culture over the individual. He said that there is a special *superorganic sphere of culture*. **Emile Durkheim** proposed that a new social science rooted in the collective consciousness and social facts be developed. He felt that anthropologists should be examining individuals only in the context of their larger social system.

Cultural Ecology

Cultural ecology or ecological anthropology first surfaced as a theoretical perspective in the 1950s. It is the examination of how humans acclimate to the environments and how in turn culture is used to preserve their ecosystems. Inherent to these studies is awareness of the particular society's environmental systems and perceptions, known as their **ethnoecology**. **Environmental anthropology** is a contemporary term for ecological anthropology. Today, escalating emphasis on globalization and environmental issues can lead to implementation of measures that are at odds with local autonomy and livelihood. This makes a **cultural ecology** perspective particularly relevant currently.

Symbolic and Interpretive Anthropology

These are two closely related schools of thought that both emphasize the importance of symbols in cultures. **Symbolic anthropology** is the analysis of symbols in the social and cultural framework. It was promoted primarily by Victor Turner and Mary Douglas. **Interpretive anthropology**, whose primary proponent was Clifford Geertz, looks at cultures as systems with meanings that need to be decoded within the framework of history and the culture. These meanings can be gleaned by examination of any public types of symbols, which can include things like societal rituals and customs as well as words.

Theoretical Approaches That Emphasize the Process

Today there is increasing emphasis among anthropologists on the process of cultural change or **agency**. Agency means the measures that individuals, acting alone or collectively, take to create and change cultural identities. Two approaches emphasizing the process are practice theory and action theory. **Practice theory** contends that culture influences people's experiences and responses, but individuals can also actively participate in societal change within their own constraints. **Active theory**, primarily espoused by Edmund Leach, marries structural functionalism with the creative process by which individuals obtain power and thus alter culture.

Additional Theoretical Approaches

A number of investigators have considered a historical approach called **world-system theory**. This perspective basically says that many cultural changes were prompted by the increasing political economy and the spread of capitalism. **Political economy** is the network of interconnected economic and other influential forces resulting from the ability to interact with other cultures through trade or other interactions. Some other approaches consider sources of power to be influential on culture and history. Gramsci promoted the idea of **hegemony**, in which underlings accept and acquiesce to a ruler because they consider it natural. Other modern anthropologists have taken similar views, stressing that power is achieved not only through physical aggression but also by dominating people's minds.

The Sociological Perspective

Interpreting Maps

The **map legend** is an area that provides interpretation information such as the key, the scale, and how to interpret the map. The **key** is the area that defines symbols, abbreviations, and color schemes used on the map. Any feature identified on the map should be defined in the key. The **scale** is a feature of the map legend that tells how distance on the map relates to distance on the ground. It can either be presented mathematically in a ratio or visually with a line segment. For example, it could say that one inch on the map equals one foot on the ground, or it could show a line segment and tell how much distance on the map the line symbolizes. **Latitude** and **longitude** are often shown on maps to relate their area to the world. Latitude shows how far a location is north or south from the earth's equator, and longitude shows how far a location is east or west from the earth's prime meridian. Latitude runs from 90 N (North Pole) – 0 (equator) – 90 S (South Pole), and longitude runs 180 E (international date line) – 0 (prime meridian) – 180 W (international date line).

Review Video: <u>5 Elements of any Map</u>
Visit mometrix.com/academy and enter code: 437727

Popular Map Projections

- **Globe**: Earth's features are shown on a sphere. No distortion of distances, directions, or areas occurs.
- **Mercator**: projects Earth's features onto a cylinder wrapped around a globe. Generates a rectangular map that is not distorted at the equator but is greatly distorted near the poles. Lines of latitude and longitude form a square grid.
- **Robinson**: projects Earth's features onto an oval-looking map. Areas near the poles are truer to size than in the Mercator. Some distortion affects every point.
- **Orthographic**: Earth's features are shown on a circle, which is tangent to the globe at any point chosen by the mapmaker. Generates a circular, 3D-appearing map similar to how Earth is seen from space.
- **Conic maps**: A family of maps drawn by projecting the globe's features onto a cone set onto the globe. Some distortion affects most points.
- **Polar maps**: A circle onto which the land around the poles has been projected. Provides much less distortion of Antarctica and the land around the North Pole than other map types.

Cartographic Distortion and its Influence on Map Projections

Cartographic distortion is the distortion caused by projecting a three-dimensional structure, in this case the surface of the earth, onto the two-dimensional surface of a map. Numerous map projections have been developed to minimize distortion, but the only way to eliminate distortion completely is to render the earth in three dimensions. Most map projections have minimal distortion in some location, usually the center, and the distortion becomes greater close to the edges of the map. Some map projections try to compromise and distribute the distortion more evenly across the map. Different categories of maps preserve, or do not distort, different features. Maps that preserve directions accurately are **azimuthal**, and maps that preserve shapes properly are **conformal**. Area-preserving maps are called **equal-area maps**, and maps that preserve

50

distance are called **distance-preserving**. Maps that preserve the shortest routes are **gnomonic projections**.

Comparing Maps of the Same Place from Different Time Periods

Maps of the same place from different time periods can often be initially aligned by **geographic features**. Political and land-use boundaries are most likely to change between time periods, whereas locations of waterways and geologic features such as mountains are relatively constant. Once geographic features have been used to align maps, they can be compared side-by-side to examine the changing locations of human settlement, smaller waterways, etc. This kind of map interpretation, at the smallest scale, provides information about how small groups of humans **interact with their environment**. For example, such analysis might show that major cities began around ports, and then moved inland as modes of transportation, like railroads and cars, became more common. Lands that were initially used for agriculture might become incorporated into a nearby city as the population grows. This kind of map analysis can also show the evolution of the **socio-economics** of an area, providing information about the relative importance of economic activities (manufacturing, agriculture or trade) and even the commuting behavior of workers.

Natural, Political, and Cultural Features on Maps

Map legends will provide information about the types of natural, political, or cultural features on a map. Some maps show only one of these three features. **Natural features** such as waterways, wetlands, beaches, deserts, mountains, highlands and plains can be compared between regions by type, number, distribution, or any other physical characteristic. **Political features** such as state and county divisions or roads and railroads can be compared numerically, but examining their geographic distribution may be more informative. This provides information on settlement density and population. In addition, road and railroad density may show regions of intense urbanization, agricultural regions, or industrial centers. **Cultural features** may include roads and railroads, but might also include historic areas, museums, archaeological digs, early settlements and even campgrounds. Comparing and contrasting the number, distribution, and types of these features may provide information on the history of an area, the duration of settlement of an area, or the current use of the area (for example, many museums are found in current-day cultural centers).

Comparing Maps with Datasets or Texts

Maps can provide a great deal of information about an area by showing specific locations where certain types of settlement, land use, or population growth occurred. **Datasets** and **texts** can provide more specific information about events that can be hypothesized from maps. This specific information may provide dates of significant events (for example, the date of a fire that gutted a downtown region, forcing suburban development) or important numerical data (e.g., population growth by year). Written datasets and texts enable map interpretation to become concrete and allow observed trends to be linked with specific causes ("Real estate prices rose in 2004, causing middle-class citizens to move northwest of the city"). Without specific information from additional sources, inferences drawn from maps cannot be put in **context** and interpreted in more than a vague way.

Mometrix

Evaluating Graphic Formats

The type of information being conveyed guides the choice of **format**. Textual information and numeric information must be displayed with different techniques. Text-only information may be most easily summarized in a diagram or a timeline. If text includes numeric information, it may be converted into a chart that shows the size of groups, connects ideas in a table or graphic, or shows information in a hybridized format. Ideas or opinions can be effectively conveyed in political cartoons. Numeric information is often most helpfully presented in tables or graphs. When information will be referred to and looked up again and again, tables are often most helpful for the reader. When the trends in the numeric information are more important than the numbers themselves, graphs are often the best choice. Information that is linked to the land and has a spatial component is best conveyed using maps.

Using Electronic Resources and Periodicals for Reference

Electronic resources are often the quickest, most convenient way to get background information on a topic. One of the particular strengths of **electronic resources** is that they can also provide primary-source multimedia video, audio, or other visual information on a topic that would not be accessible in print. Information available on the Internet is not often carefully screened for accuracy or for bias, so choosing the **source** of electronic information is often very important. Electronic encyclopedias can provide excellent overview information, but publicly edited resources like Wikipedia are open to error, rapid change, incompleteness, or bias. Students should be made aware of the different types and reliabilities of electronic resources, and they should be taught how to distinguish between them. Electronic resources can often be too detailed and overwhelm students with irrelevant information. **Periodicals** provide current information on social science events, but they too must be screened for bias. Some amount of identifiable bias can actually be an important source of information, because it indicates prevailing culture and standards. Periodicals generally have tighter editorial standards than electronic resources, so completeness and overt errors are not usually as problematic. Periodicals can also provide primary-source information with interviews and photographs.

Using Encyclopedias, bibliographies, or Almanacs for Social Science Research

Encyclopedias are ideal for getting background information on a topic. They provide an overview of the topic, and link it to other concepts that can provide additional keywords, information, or subjects. They can help students narrow their topic by showing the sub-topics within the overall topic, and by relating it to other topics. **Encyclopedias** are often more useful than the Internet because they provide a clearly organized, concise overview of material. **Bibliographies** are bound collections of references to periodicals and books, organized by topic. Students can begin researching more efficiently after they identify a topic, look it up in a bibliography, and look up the references listed there. This provides a branching network of information a student can follow. A pitfall of bibliographies is that when in textbooks or other journal articles, the references in them are chosen to support the author's point of view, and so may be limited in scope. **Almanacs** are volumes of facts published annually. They provide numerical information on just about every topic, and are organized by subject or geographic region. They are often helpful for supporting arguments made using other resources, and do not provide any interpretation of their own.

Primary and Secondary Resources

Primary resources provide information about an event from the perspective of people who were present at the event. They might be letters, autobiographies, interviews, speeches, artworks, or

52

anything created by people with first-hand experience. **Primary resources** are valuable because they provide not only facts about the event, but also information about the surrounding circumstances; for example, a letter might provide commentary about how a political speech was received. The Internet is a source of primary information, but care must be taken to evaluate the perspective of the website providing that information. Websites hosted by individuals or special-interest organizations are more likely to be biased than those hosted by public organizations, governments, educational institutions, or news associations.

Secondary resources provide information about an event, but were not written at the time the event occurred. They draw information from primary sources. Because secondary sources were written later, they have the added advantage of historical perspective, multiple points of view, or resultant outcomes. Newsmagazines that write about an event even a week after it occurred count as secondary sources. Secondary sources tend to analyze events more effectively or thoroughly than primary sources.

Formulating Research Questions or Hypotheses

Formulating research questions or hypotheses is the process of finding questions to answer that have not yet been asked. The first step in the process is reading **background information**. Knowing about a general topic and reading about how other people have addressed it helps identify areas that are well understood. Areas that are not as well understood may either be lightly addressed in the available literature, or distinctly identified as a topic that is not well understood and deserves further study. Research questions or hypotheses may address such an unknown aspect, or they may focus on drawing parallels between similar, well-researched topics that have not been connected before. Students usually need practice in developing research questions that are of the appropriate scope so that they will find enough information to answer the question, yet not so much that they become overwhelmed. Hypotheses tend to be more specific than research questions.

Collecting Information, Organizing and Reporting Results

The first step of writing a research paper involves narrowing down on a **topic**. The student should first read background information to identify areas that are interesting or need further study and that the student does not have a strong opinion about. The research question should be identified, and the student should refer to general sources that can point to more specific information. When he begins to take notes, his information must be **organized** with a clear system to identify the source. Any information from outside sources must be acknowledged with **footnotes** or a **bibliography**. To gain more specific information about his topic, the student can then research bibliographies of the general sources to narrow down on information pertinent to his topic. He should draft a thesis statement that summarizes the main point of the research. This should lead to a working **outline** that incorporates all the ideas needed to support the main point in a logical order. A rough draft should incorporate the results of the research in the outlined order, with all citations clearly inserted. The paper should then be edited for clarity, style, flow, and content.

Analyzing Artifacts

Artifacts, or everyday objects used by previous cultures, are useful for understanding life in those cultures. Students should first discover, or be provided with, a **description** of the item. This description should tell during what period the **artifact** was used and what culture used it. From that description and/or from examination of the artifact, students should be able to discuss what the artifact is, what it is made of, its potential uses, and the people who likely used it. They should

53

then be able to draw **conclusions** from all these pieces of evidence about life in that culture. For example, analysis of coins from an early American archaeological site might show that settlers brought coins with them, or that some classes of residents were wealthy, or that trade occurred with many different nations. The interpretation will vary depending on the circumstances surrounding the artifact. Students should consider these circumstances when drawing conclusions.

Identifying Main Ideas in a Document

Main ideas in a paragraph are often found in the **topic sentence**, which is usually the first or second sentence in the paragraph. Every following sentence in the paragraph should relate to that initial information. Sometimes, the first or second sentence doesn't obviously set up the main idea. When that happens, each sentence in the paragraph should be read carefully to find the **common theme** between them all. This common theme is the main idea of the paragraph. Main ideas in an entire document can be found by analyzing the structure of the document. Frequently, the document begins with an introductory paragraph or abstract that will summarize the main ideas. Each paragraph often discusses one of the main ideas and contributes to the overall goal of the document. Some documents are divided up into chapters or sections, each of which discusses a main idea. The way that main ideas are described in a document (either in sentences, paragraphs, or chapters) depends on the length of the document.

Organizing Information Chronologically and Analyzing the Sequence of Events

To organize information chronologically, each piece of information must be associated with a time or a date. Events are ordered according to the time or date at which they happened. In social sciences, chronological organization is the most straightforward way to arrange information, because it relies on a uniform, fixed scale – the passage of time. Information can also be organized based on any of the "who, what, when, where, why?" principles.

Analyzing the sequence of chronological events involves not only examining the event itself, but the preceding and following events. This can put the event in question into perspective, showing how a certain thing might have happened based on preceding history. One large disadvantage of chronological organization is that it may not highlight important events clearly relative to less important events. Determining the relative importance of events depends more strongly on interpreting their relationships to neighboring events.

Recognizing Cause-and-Effect Relationships, and Comparing Similarities and Differences

Cause-and-effect relationships are simply linkages between an event that happened (the **effect**) because of some other event (the **cause**). Effects are always chronologically ordered after causes. Effects can be found by asking why something happened, or looking for information following words like so, consequently, since, because, therefore, this led to, as a result, and thus. Causes can be found by asking what happened. **Comparing similarities and differences** involves mentally setting two concepts next to each other and then listing the ways they are the same and the ways they are different. The level of comparison varies by student level; for example, younger students may compare the physical characteristics of two animals while older students compare the themes of a book. Similarity/difference comparisons can be done by listing written descriptions in a point-by-point approach, or they can be done in several graphic ways. Venn diagrams are commonly used to organize information, showing non-overlapping clouds filled with information about the different characteristics of A and B, and the overlapping area shows ways in which A and B are the same. Idea maps using arrows and bubbles can also be developed to show these differences.

Distinguishing Between Fact and Opinion

Students easily recognize that **facts** are true statements that everyone agrees on, such as an object's name or a statement about a historical event. Students also recognize that **opinions** vary about matters of taste, such as preferences in food or music, that rely on people's interpretation of facts. Simple examples are easy to spot. **Fact-based passages** include certainty-grounded words like is, did, or saw. On the other hand, **passages containing opinions** often include words that indicate possibility rather than certainty, such as would, should or believe. First-person verbs also indicate opinions, showing that one person is talking about his experience. Less clear are examples found in higher-level texts. For example, primary-source accounts of a Civil War battle might include facts ("X battle was fought today") and also opinions ("Union soldiers are not as brave as Confederate soldiers") that are not clearly written as such ("I believe Union soldiers..."). At the same time as students learn to interpret sources critically (Was the battle account written by a Southerner?), they should practice sifting fact from these types of opinion. Other examples where fact and opinion blend together are self-authored internet websites.

> **Review Video:** Fact or Opinion
> Visit mometrix.com/academy and enter code: 870899

Determining the Adequacy, Relevance, and Consistency of Information

Before information is sought, a list of **guiding questions** should be developed to help determine whether information found is adequate, relevant, and consistent. These questions should be based on the **research goals**, which should be laid out in an outline or concept map. For example, a student writing a report on Navajo social structure might begin with questions concerning the general lifestyle and location of Navajos, and follow with questions about how Navajo society was organized. While researching his questions, he will come up with pieces of information. This information can be compared to his research questions to determine whether it is **relevant** to his report. Information from several sources should be compared to determine whether information is **consistent**. Information that is **adequate** helps answer specific questions that are part of the research goals. Inadequate information for this particular student might be a statement such as "Navajos had a strong societal structure," because the student is probably seeking more specific information.

Drawing Conclusions and Making Generalizations About a Topic

Students reading about a topic will encounter different facts and opinions that contribute to their overall impression of the material. The student can critically examine the material by thinking about what facts have been included, how they have been presented, what they show, what they relate to outside the written material, and what the author's conclusion is. Students may agree or disagree with the author's conclusion, based on the student's interpretation of the facts the author presented. When working on a research project, a student's research questions will help him gather details that will enable him to **draw a conclusion** about the research material.

Generalizations are blanket statements that apply to a wide number of examples. They are similar to conclusions, but do not have to summarize the information as completely as conclusions. Generalizations in reading material may be flagged by words such as all, most, none, many, several, sometimes, often, never, overall, or in general. Generalizations are often followed by supporting information consisting of a list of facts. Generalizations can refer to facts or the author's opinions, and they provide a valuable summary of the text overall.

55

Interpreting Charts and Tables

Charts used in social science are a visual representation of data. They combine graphic and textual elements to convey information in a concise format. Often, **charts** divide the space up in blocks, which are filled with text and/or pictures to convey a point. Charts are often organized in tabular form, where blocks below a heading all have information in common. Charts also divide information into conceptual, non-numeric groups (for example, "favorite color"), which are then plotted against a numerical axis (e.g., "number of students"). Charts should be labeled in such a way that a reader can locate a point on the chart and then consult the surrounding axes or table headings to understand how it compares to other points. **Tables** are a type of chart that divides textual information into rows and columns. Each row and column represents a characteristic of the information. For example, a table might be used to convey demographic information. The first column would provide "year," and the second would provide "population." Reading across the rows, one could see that in the year 1966, the population of Middletown was 53,847. Tracking the columns would show how frequently the population was counted.

Interpret Graphs and Diagrams

Graphs are similar to charts, except that they graphically show numeric information on both axes. For example, a **graph** might show population through the years, with years on the X-axis and population on the Y-axis. One advantage of graphs is that population during the time in between censuses can be estimated by locating that point on the graph. Each axis should be labeled to allow the information to be interpreted correctly, and the graph should have an informative title.

Diagrams are usually drawings that show the progression of events. The drawings can be fairly schematic, as in a flow chart, or they can be quite detailed, as in a depiction of scenes from a battle. Diagrams usually have arrows connecting the events or boxes shown. Each event or box should be labeled to show what it represents. Diagrams are interpreted by following the progression along the arrows through all events.

> **Review Video: Terminology for Tables and Graphs**
> Visit mometrix.com/academy and enter code: 355505
>
> **Review Video: Understanding Charts and Tables**
> Visit mometrix.com/academy and enter code: 882112

Using Timelines in Social Science

Timelines are used to show the relationships between people, places, and events. They are ordered chronologically, and usually are shown left-to-right or top-to-bottom. Each event on the **timeline** is associated with a date, which determines its location on the timeline. On electronic resources, timelines often contain hyperlinks associated with each event. Clicking on the event's hyperlink will open a page with more information about the event. **Cause-and-effect relationships** can be observed on timelines, which often show a key event and then resulting events following in close succession. These can be helpful for showing the order of events in time or the relationships between similar events. They help make the passage of time a concrete concept, and show that large periods pass between some events, and other events cluster very closely.

Using Political Cartoons in Social Science Studies

Political cartoons are drawings that memorably convey an opinion. These opinions may be supportive or critical, and may summarize a series of events or pose a fictional situation that

56

summarizes an attitude. **Political cartoons** are therefore secondary sources of information that provide social and cultural context about events. Political cartoons may have captions that help describe the action or put it in context. They may also have dialogue, labels, or other recognizable cultural symbols. For example, Uncle Sam frequently appears in political cartoons to represent the United States Government. Political cartoons frequently employ caricature to call attention to a situation or a person. The nature of the caricature helps show the cartoonist's attitude toward the issue being portrayed. Every element of the cartoon is included to support the artist's point, and should be considered in the cartoon's interpretation. When interpreting political cartoons, students should examine what issue is being discussed, what elements the artist chose to support his or her point, and what the message is. Considering who might agree or disagree with the cartoon is also helpful in determining the message of the cartoon.

CLEP Practice Test

1. The best definition of culture is:
   a. The actual expression of societal norms
   b. The ideal of what should occur in a particular society
   c. The universal practices evident in all societies
   d. The sum of everything learned by participants in a society
   e. The most common traits among all members of a society

2. An accurate definition of society is:
   a. The most basic group in which humans and animals operate
   b. A group which values working together above all else
   c. A stated expectation of all members of a group
   d. An expectation considered to be vital to a group's welfare
   e. The usual manner of doing things according to tradition

3. Which of the following best characterizes ethnocentrism?
   a. The conviction that one's personal culture is superior to others
   b. The conviction that it is difficult to adapt to a new culture
   c. The conviction that some cultures pre-date others
   d. The conviction that matriarchal societies are superior
   e. The conviction one's personal culture is inferior to others

4. According to George Murdock, which of the following is not a general characteristic of all cultural practices?
   a. Religion
   b. Folklore
   c. Property disputes
   d. Tool-making
   e. Laws

5. Which of the following values is not identifiable in American culture?
   a. A respect for education for all
   b. A respect for philosophical thinking
   c. A respect for progress
   d. A respect for moderation in everything
   e. A respect for humanitarianism

6. All societies contain certain basic institutions. Which of the following is excluded from these basic institutions?
   a. Education
   b. Government
   c. Economic
   d. Religious
   e. Medical

58

7. Stating that Americans begin families after marriage, when in fact they often have children outside the institution of marriage, is an example of:

    a. Stratification
    b. Subculture
    c. Counter-culture
    d. Patterned evasion
    e. Secularism

8. The following statements are true of all societies with the exception of:

    a. Societies are where culture takes place
    b. Societies are interdependent for the mutual survival of all
    c. Members of a society live in a specific area
    d. Sexual reproduction is the chief means of continuing a society
    e. A primary method of organizing a society is according to labor tasks

9. Which of the following does not exemplify a typical response to rapid change?

    a. Culture shock
    b. Future shock
    c. Cultural lag
    d. Societal lag
    e. Patterned evasion

10. Many airports have not been improved so that they can accommodate advances in aviation. This is due to:

    a. Future shock
    b. Cultural lag
    c. Culture shock
    d. Cultural configuration
    e. Technological rush

11. A sampling method used in survey research which relies upon established differences in populations is known as:

    a. Stratified sampling
    b. Role sampling
    c. Systematic sampling
    d. Representative sampling
    e. Correlational sampling

12. All of the following processes represent stages of sociological research with the exception of:

    a. Identification of the problem to be studied
    b. Selection and review of pertinent literature
    c. Selection of the individual to be studied
    d. Identification of research design
    e. Formulating a hypothesis

13. Which of these definitions best describes qualitative methods used in sociological research?

    a. Research methods which focus on measurement
    b. Research methods which focus on statistics
    c. Research methods which focus on quantification
    d. Research methods which focus on studying change
    e. Research methods which focus on personal observations

14. Content analysis does not include the study of which of the following?

    a. Averages
    b. Means
    c. Percentages
    d. Modes
    e. Redundancy

15. Which of the problems listed below does not provide an ethical dilemma for sociologists?

    a. Invasion of privacy of the group
    b. Method of application of research
    c. Possibility of harm to participants
    d. Issues of individual consent
    e. Full disclosure skewing research results

16. Which of these theorists is credited with the founding of psychoanalysis?

    a. Sigmund Freud
    b. George Herbert Mead
    c. Charles Horton Cooley
    d. Jean Piaget
    e. Erving Goffman

17. According to Jean Piaget, all of the following phases are a part of cognitive development with the exception of:

    a. The sensorimotor phase
    b. The abstract operational phase
    c. The preoperational phase
    d. The concrete operational phase
    e. The formal operational phase

18. _____ names a marriage in which one wife is simultaneously married to two or more husbands.

    a. Group marriage
    b. Patrilocality
    c. Polyandry
    d. Nuclearity
    e. Ritualism

19. According to Max Weber, which group reflects the fundamental organization of all societies?
    a. A reference group
    b. An in-group
    c. A bureaucracy
    d. A characteristic institution
    e. Nuclear group

20. Which of the following stages is not a recognized research stage?
    a. Identifying the problem to be studied
    b. Finding the appropriate design for research
    c. Screening the subjects
    d. Explaining the final conclusion of the study
    e. Selection and review of pertinent literature

21. In a/an _____ society, the major focus is upon information, rather than upon material goods.
    a. Hunting and gathering
    b. Post-industrial
    c. Horticultural
    d. Agricultural
    e. Ideological

22. If a man is concurrently described as being a psychologist, a husband, a father, and a respected member of the community, he is being defined according to his:
    a. Ascribed status
    b. Master status
    c. Achieved status
    d. Status set
    e. Salient status

23. All of the descriptions listed below are characteristics of deviance with the exception of which one?
    a. It offers encouragement that societal controls work
    b. It often correlates with high intelligence
    c. It often correlates with mental illness
    d. It often correlates with criminal behavior
    e. It often correlates with great ambition

24. The nursing profession is an example of which of the following sectors?
    a. The predominant sector
    b. The economic sector
    c. The social sector
    d. The distributive sector
    e. The tertiary sector

25. Which of the following types of government has leaders who fail to recognize the limitations of their authority?
    a. Authoritarian
    b. Totalitarian
    c. Democratic
    d. Systematic
    e. Problematic

26. According to Max Weber, what are the major categories of authority?
    I. Traditional authority
    II. Rational-legal authority
    III. Charismatic authority
    IV. Democratic authority
    a. I, II, and III only
    b. I, III, and IV only
    c. II, III, and IV only
    d. I, II, and IV only
    e. I, II, III, and IV

27. Religion is not associated with which of the following societal functions?
    a. Theodicy
    b. Theocracy
    c. Codes of ethics
    d. Personality
    e. Historical condition

28. Typical sources of stratification do not include:
    a. Race
    b. Age
    c. Gender
    d. Sexual preference
    e. Social status

29. Which of the following characteristics are not exhibited by collective behavior?
    a. Fashion
    b. Spontaneity
    c. Stereotypes
    d. Instability
    e. Revolution

30. According to C. Wright Mills, some examples of the power elite include all of the following with the exception of:
    a. Business executives
    b. High-ranking military officers
    c. Elected representatives
    d. College professors
    e. Appointed judges

31. Which of the following are not qualities of participants in social groups?
    a. They tend to interrelate systematically
    b. They tend to display similar qualities
    c. They exhibit a mutual tendency towards awareness
    d. They tend to join on a voluntary or involuntary basis
    e. They tend to be interdependent

32. The major features of a/an _____ society are the use of hand tools to cultivate plants and the domestication of animals:
    a. Horticultural and pastoral
    b. Agricultural
    c. Hunting and gathering
    d. Industrial
    e. Postindustrial

33. Which of the following statements does not describe an agricultural society?
    a. This society is more technologically advanced than horticultural and pastoral societies.
    b. Irrigation is an important tool for this society.
    c. Draft animals are of considerable importance in this society.
    d. It is impossible to have a big surplus in this society.
    e. Permanent tools necessary for survival.

34. All of the following descriptions are typical of an industrial society with the exception of:
    a. Machines are employed for production purposes
    b. Energy sources are employed for production purposes
    c. Autos were developed in this society
    d. The principal focus of this society is gathering information
    e. Radios were popularized by this society

35. Sociocultural evolution:
    a. Describes the inclination of cultures to increase in complexity in the long run
    b. Describes the interconnection which exists between people
    c. Describes the quantity of cultural elements which are environmentally based
    d. Describes a specific method of categorizing societies
    e. Describes the change in language and art of a culture as it progresses

36. Of the following statements, which one is not true of social mobility?
    a. It is sometimes relative
    b. It is sometimes absolute
    c. It can involve proceeding through various levels of social stratification
    d. It is normally unrelated to structural mobility
    e. It is relatively unhindered in an open stratification system

37. Which of the characteristics mentioned below is not typical of social inequality?
    a. Different treatment because of sex
    b. Different treatment because of health
    c. Different treatment because of race
    d. Different treatment because of age
    e. Different treatment because of religion

38. All of the following are recognized distinctions often leading to differential treatment in societies with the exception of:
    a. Gender differences
    b. Age differences
    c. Religious differences
    d. Compatibility differences
    e. Racial differences

39. In general, sociologists have found that people from similar social strata share the following features except:
    a. They have similar opportunities in life
    b. They benefit equally from societal advantages
    c. They are affected similarly by societal disadvantages
    d. They generally participate in social stratification
    e. They generally attempt to be socially mobile

40. Which of these sociologists subscribe to a functionalist view of social stratification?
    I. Max Weber
    II. Karl Marx
    III. Kingsley Davis
    IV. Wilbert Moore
    V. David Riesman
    a. III and IV only
    b. I and V only
    c. II and V only
    d. I and II only
    e. I, II, III, and IV

41. A grown daughter's living standards have improved beyond those of her mother. This is an example of:
    a. Social hierarchy
    b. Absolute mobility
    c. Relative mobility
    d. Social stratification
    e. Social mobility

42. An inescapable consequence of social stratification is:
    a. Social mobility
    b. Absolute mobility
    c. Social hierarchy
    d. Social injustice
    e. Social inequality

43. The sociologist who defines modern conflict theory according to educational credentials is:
    a. Karl Marx
    b. Randall Collins
    c. Ralf Dahrendorf
    d. Max Weber
    e. Kingsley Davis

44. In the past century, the most conclusive theories regarding how unusual collective behavior is defined includes the:

      I. Contagion theory
      II. Emergent-image theory
      III. Confluence theory
      IV. Convergence theory
      V. Emergent-norm theory

  a. I, IV, and V only
  b. I, II, and III only
  c. III, IV, and V only
  d. I, II, and V only
  e. II, IV, and V only

45. The founders of the emergent-norm theory are:

      I. Gustave LeBon
      II. Rodney King
      III. Ralph Turner
      IV. Karl Marx
      V. Lewis Killian

  a. III and V only
  b. IV and V only
  c. II and V only
  d. I and II only
  e. I, II, and III

46. The father of the contagion theory is:

  a. Lewis Killian
  b. Gustave LeBon
  c. Ralph Turner
  d. Karl Marx
  e. Ralf Dahrendorf

47. A teenager's high school friends pressure him to get drunk. If he succumbs to the pressure his behavior can be seen as an example of:

  a. Convergence theory
  b. Emergent-norm theory
  c. Survival of the fittest theory
  d. Contagion theory
  e. Exchange theory

48. Convergence theory:

  a. Proposes that sociologists, like psychologists, are influenced by their own incentives
  b. Proposes that a person is influenced more by his/her own incentives than by the group's incentives
  c. Proposes that social stratification is influenced most by its own incentives
  d. Proposes that economic change is influenced most by its own incentives
  e. Proposes that the upper classes are influenced most by their own incentives

49. An illustration of the emergent-norm theory in action is:

    a. An adult shoots a thief, and others fire their own shots shortly thereafter

    b. A crowd storms through town to defend a wounded soldier

    c. A father becomes threatened because his son is more successful than he is

    d. A child attempts to convince a group that violence is wrong

    e. A stadium audience starts booing a protester who stormed the field

50. Which of the characteristics listed below is true of riots?

    a. They reflect a "keep-up-with-the-Joneses" mentality

    b. They reflect a strong influence from peer envy

    c. They take more time to complete than mob actions

    d. They are more prone to violence than mob actions

    e. Spread of social contagion is always based in fact

51. Which of the problem(s) listed below would not pose an ethical problem for sociologists who are performing research?

    I. Concern about deceiving the individual

    II. Concern about harm to the subjects studied

    III. Concern about proper application of research results

    IV. Concern about risks to the individual

    V. Concern about participants' consent

    a. II and III only

    b. III and V only

    c. I and IV only

    d. I only

    e. II, III, and V only

52. According to Sigmund Freud, which statement is not true as regards personality?

    a. There are three key elements which shape personality

    b. Consciousness is actually equated with the ego

    c. The id provides a system of checks and balances for the ego

    d. Identification is essential to personality development

    e. Repression is crucial to personality development

53. Which of the following statements do not reflect George Herbert Mead's beliefs about socialization?

    a. He believed that socialization leads to facility in identifying deviant behavior

    b. He believed that socialization results in a predictive facility as regards human reactions

    c. He believed that socialization results in adaptive abilities as regards human behavior

    d. He believed that socialization results in facility in modeling human behavior

    e. He believed that socialization involves a significant other and a generalized other

54. According to Erving Goffman, which of the following statements is not true?

    a. The formation of the self is strongly correlated with feedback given by others

    b. The formation of the self strongly reflects multiple human interactions

    c. The formation of the self is strongly influenced by one's attempts to sway others

    d. The differences between the authentic self and the public portrayal of self are known as role-distance

    e. The dramaturgical approach involves controlling the way others perceive a person

55. Charles Horton Cooley espoused all of the theories below with the exception of:
    a. The self-concept is established early in life
    b. The self-concept is fragile and easily damaged
    c. The self-concept undergoes constant reassessment
    d. The self-concept is acquired through a "looking glass"
    e. The self-concept is developed based on the treatment one receives from other members of society

56. Which of the following phases are not included in Erik Erikson's phases of ego formation?
    a. The nurturing phase
    b. The young adult phase
    c. The change from home-to-school phase
    d. The seasoned adult phase
    e. The rebellious teenage phase

57. Which of the following statements does not describe Lawrence Kohlberg's theories?
    a. He believed that moral reasoning evolves through six basic steps
    b. He was strongly influenced by Jean Piaget
    c. He was thought to be short-sighted in regards to women
    d. He believed that adolescence was a key step in the development of morals
    e. Moral reasoning is constant throughout one's life

58. Which of the statements below does not describe Carol Gilligan's viewpoint?
    a. Women tend to deal with ethical challenges via a perspective of responsibility
    b. Men tend to deal with ethical challenges via a perspective of ultimate results
    c. Boys and girls present substantial differences as to how their psyches operate
    d. The two sexes approach problem-solving differently because of their divergent societal roles
    e. Pre-pubescent children's psyches operate similarly and diverge after puberty

59. _____ is the societal custom in which a husband simultaneously has two or more wives.
    a. Polygyny
    b. Kinship
    c. Group marriage
    d. Patrilocality
    e. Mormonism

60. Which of the following statements is false in regards to deviance?
    a. A social group can frequently become united as a result of deviance
    b. Clear boundaries of appropriate behavior are delineated by deviance
    c. A reasonable method of protest is provided through deviance
    d. Both formal and informal controls over society are provided by deviance
    e. A significant result of deviance is that it often destroys a group

61. _____ is a simultaneous marriage between multiple women and multiple men.

   a. Monogamy
   b. Group marriage
   c. Mormonism
   d. Mutual consent
   e. Polygyny

62. The fact that Americans forbid marriage between immediate family members is an example of:

   a. Monogamy
   b. Polygamy
   c. Exogamy
   d. Kinship
   e. Nuclearity

63. If the authority of the family rests with the mother, this is an example of a:

   a. Matriarchy
   b. Matrilocality
   c. Matrilineal society
   d. Matrimonial society
   e. Matricentric society

64. All of the following describe a patriarchy except:

   a. It is sometimes matrilineal
   b. It is sometimes matrilocal
   c. The levirate is sometimes present in this society
   d. Primogeniture is sometimes present in this society
   e. Father-rule is not necessary

65. A _____ society is one in which the family's authority rests primarily with the father.

   a. Patrimonial
   b. Patrilineal
   c. Patronizing
   d. Patriarchal
   e. Paternal

66. _____ is the societal custom in which marriage is only permitted between individuals belonging to the same, or similar, groups.

   a. Endogamy
   b. Nuclearity
   c. Integration
   d. Monogamy
   e. Polyandry

67. If a person marries once, later divorces, and then marries once again, this is an example of:

   a. Polygamy
   b. Serial monogamy
   c. Deviance
   d. Matrimony
   e. Stigma

68. A father from a patriarchal society who passes on his property to his youngest son is practicing:
    a. Ultimogeniture
    b. Primogeniture
    c. Neolocality
    d. Patrilocality
    e. Parsimony

69. A pattern of tracing family lineage through the mother's side of the family is an example of _____ research.
    a. Matrilocal
    b. Matriarchal
    c. Matrilineal
    d. Matrimonial
    e. Maternal

70. According to Edwin Sutherland, all of the following statements are true except:
    a. Primary groups are the breeding grounds for criminal behavior.
    b. Social interaction is a means by which criminal behavior is learned.
    c. Childhood is often the time of life in which people learn to be criminals.
    d. Criminal behavior is tied to a belief in its advantages.
    e. Criminal behavior is found more prevalently in people in the lower class.

71. The teaching profession has recently evolved such that it now requires the presentation of technical material. However, this profession remains at a similar level socially. Thus, the teaching profession today is an example of:
    a. Relative stratification
    b. Relative mobility
    c. Relative orientation
    d. Relative structure
    e. Relative status

72. Social stratification terminology includes all of the following except:
    a. False consciousness
    b. Status attainment theory
    c. Visibility
    d. Caste system
    e. Social bonds

73. All of the following statements are interpretations of the bases of modern conflict theory with the exception of:
    a. It can be based upon conflicts between different groups.
    b. It can be based upon ideological differences.
    c. It can be based upon a struggle to acquire educational credentials.
    d. It can be based upon an individual's struggles for self-awareness.
    e. It can be based upon the struggle between individual desire and societal norms.

74. Which of the following has a charismatic leader, voluntary membership, and reflects the most basic type of organizational structure possible?

  a. Church
  b. Sect
  c. Cult
  d. Fad
  e. Civil religion

75. All of the characteristics presented below describe a church, with the exception of:

  a. It has a formal leader
  b. Its membership is based upon social stratification
  c. It is recognized as an institution
  d. It is only possible to abandon membership involuntarily
  e. It exists in a low state of tension with surrounding society

76. Which of the following traits do not reflect faiths based in East Asia and parts of Southeast Asia?

  a. They emphasize the teaching and learning of religious doctrines.
  b. They emphasize the value of self-understanding.
  c. They value nature.
  d. They revere multiple gods.
  e. They did not originate with Abraham.

77. Which of the following traits is not characteristic of collective behavior?

  a. It is inclined to be spontaneous
  b. It is inclined to be devoid of any support from an institution
  c. It is challenging to view it in action
  d. It rarely changes
  e. It is inclined to be unpredictable

78. Which of the following statements most accurately defines propaganda?

  a. It describes an issue of public interest
  b. It describes social stratification
  c. It describes the opinions of the public
  d. It entails efforts to alter public opinion
  e. It is purely political

79. Major studies of social problems resulting from social stratification worldwide include all of the following except:

  I. Domestic abuse
  II. Clinical depression
  III. Date rape
  IV. Adolescent pregnancies

  a. I, III, and IV only
  b. II and IV only
  c. IV only
  d. I and III only
  e. I, II, and III only

80. Which of the dimensions mentioned below does not affect social stratification?

      I. Manual
      II. Domestic
      III. Environmental
      IV. National
      V. Ideological

   a. II and V only
   b. I, IV, and V only
   c. I, II, III, and IV only
   d. II only
   e. V only

81. Of the factors listed below, which are Max Weber's independent factors associated with his theory of social stratification?

      I. Social class
      II. Personal power
      III. Social status
      IV. Race

   a. I, III, and IV only
   b. II and IV only
   c. IV only
   d. I and III only
   e. I, II, and III only

82. Max Weber believed that all of the following were fundamental classes of society with the exception of:

   a. The middle class
   b. The most affluent class
   c. The petite bourgeoisie
   d. The class of manual laborers
   e. White-collar workers

83. A supervisor who needs to be firm with employees about output and deadlines but who also likes to go bowling with them on the weekends, can been seen as an example of:

   a. Role strain
   b. Role conflict
   c. Role play
   d. Role reversal
   e. Role distance

84. Susan is a licensed psychologist. This description of Susan is her:

   a. Ascribed status
   b. Inferred status
   c. Achieved status
   d. Master status
   e. Adopted status

85. According to Ferdinand Tonnies, a good definition of gemeinschaft is:
    a. Community
    b. Society
    c. Dyad
    d. Triad
    e. Role play

86. Some major categories of groups which sociologists have traditionally studied include all with the exception of:
    a. Aggregates
    b. Families
    c. Peer groups
    d. Conglomerates
    e. Secondary groups

87. If a sociologist were to write all potential research subjects' names on individual cards, shuffle them, and then choose a certain number of cards with names which would be appropriate for a study, she is putting together a _____ sample.
    a. Representative
    b. Random
    c. Systematic
    d. Stratified
    e. Descriptive

88. When Elton May found in his studies that the sociologist's presence during research can alter the behavior of the participants, he actually discovered the _____.
    a. Control group effect
    b. Content analysis effect
    c. Random sample effect
    d. Stratification effect
    e. Hawthorne effect

89. The sociologist who is credited with discovering the grand theory of society is:
    a. Talcott Parsons
    b. Robert Merton
    c. C. Wright Mills
    d. Dennis Wong
    e. Erving Goffman

90. Which of the following is not representative of a group which is oriented towards religion?
    a. Cult
    b. Sect
    c. Church
    d. Temple
    e. Stratification

91. Which of the activities listed below is not associated with the primary sector of the economy?
    a. Hunting deer
    b. Gathering plants and herbs
    c. Panning for gold
    d. Farming
    e. Manufacturing cars

92. _____ is an activity associated with the secondary sector of the economy.
    a. Panning for gold
    b. Manufacturing weapons
    c. Providing electrical wiring
    d. Providing physical therapy
    e. Teaching Spanish

93. Robert works as an occupational therapist for the local public schools system. His profession is part of the _____ sector.
    a. Service
    b. Manufacturing
    c. Production
    d. Cultivation
    e. Free market

94. _____ is a profession associated with the primary economic sector.
    a. Knitting
    b. Making rugs
    c. Mining diamonds
    d. Mending clothes
    e. Repairing jewelry

95. The production and profitable sale of a variety of both goods and services includes which of the following economic sectors?
    I. Barter
    II. Free market
    III. Direct exchange
    IV. Supply and demand
    V. Service

    a. I and IV only
    b. II and III only
    c. V only
    d. I, III, and IV only
    e. III and V only

96. Economic distribution systems encompass all of the following with the exception of:
    a. The secondary sector
    b. The free market system
    c. The barter system
    d. The direct exchange
    e. The informal sector

97. Which of the following is not true about racial socialization?
    a. Individuals within different racial groups are socialized differently.
    b. Typically, it describes the experience of minorities within a society.
    c. It may vary between racial or ethnic groups.
    d. Only the most underprivileged races experience racial socialization.
    e. It occurs when individuals interact with the society at large.

98. Which one of the following statements is not descriptive of ethnicity?
    a. It sometimes refers to the ability of a group to move through the social strata
    b. It sometimes refers to a group recognized by its shared language.
    c. It sometimes refers to a population which shares a national heritage
    d. It is sometimes used as a means of enacting social stratification
    e. It is sometimes based on differences taught and learned in a particular culture

99. Traits associated with gender differences include all of the following with the exception of:
    a. Hairstyles
    b. Clothes
    c. Family position
    d. Professions
    e. Ethnic roles

100. Bill is a retired software engineer. At his previous job Bill earned $100,000 per year. Now that he has retired from that job, Bill is only offered a salary of $50,000 per year for the same type of work. This is an example of:
    a. Age conflict theory
    b. Age stratification
    c. Age exception
    d. Age orientation
    e. Age functionalism

Answer Key and Explanations

1. D: Culture can best be defined as the sum of everything that is learned by participating in a society. (A) is incorrect because it is the specific definition of real culture, rather than a general definition of culture itself. (B) defines ideal culture; again, this is a specific definition of a type of culture, rather than a definition of culture itself. (C) refers not to culture, but to a cultural universal. (E) is also incorrect because it is not a definition of culture.

2. A: A good definition of society is that it is the most basic group in which humans and animals operate. (B) and (C) are incorrect because they are not definitions of society. (D) is likewise wrong because it is the definition of a societal more. (E) is also incorrect because it describes a societal custom but is not a definition of society itself.

3. A: A major characteristic of ethnocentrism is the conviction that one's personal culture is the superior one. (B) is incorrect because ethnocentrism does not include the belief that it is difficult to adapt to a new culture. (C) is wrong because ethnocentrism does not reflect a conviction that some cultures pre-date others. (D) is incorrect because ethnocentrism is not associated with the belief that matriarchal societies are superior. (E) is incorrect because the correct answer is (A).

4. C: According to George Murdock, it is the preponderance of property rights, rather than property disputes, which is a characteristic of all cultural practices. It may be that property disputes arise from the characteristic of property rights, but property disputes are not, in and of themselves, one of Murdock's cultural universals. (A) is incorrect because Mr. Murdock does describe religion as a characteristic of all cultural practices. (B) is wrong because folklore is also considered a cultural universal by Murdock. (D) and (E) are incorrect because both tool-making and laws are included in Murdock's definition of cultural universals and practices.

5. B: is correct because American culture does not respect philosophical thinking. (A) is incorrect because Americans do have a respect for education for all. (C) A respect for progress, (D) a respect for moderation in everything, and (E) a respect for humanitarianism are also all incorrect answers because they represent values which are easily identifiable within American culture.

6. E: Although medical institutions are found in many societies, they are not one of the basic institutions found in all societies. (A) Educational institutions, although they can vary widely in their levels of sophistication, are common to all societies. (B) Government is another type of basic institution since all societies must organize themselves or chaos ensues. (C) and (D), economic and religious institutions, are also types of basic institutions evident in all societies.

7. D: Patterned evasion can be defined as a large discrepancy between what people claim they do and what they actually do in practice. Although Americans do have children within the context of marriage, they also have many children outside of this institution. (A) Stratification and (E) secularism are concepts unrelated to patterned evasion, as are (B) subculture and (C) counter-culture.

8. B: Interdependence among societies for the purpose of mutual survival is not a characteristic of all societies. (A) All societies are considered to be locations in which culture takes place. (C) The statements that members of a society live in a specific area, and (D) that sexual reproduction is the chief means of continuing a society are both true of all societies. (E) The statement that a primary method of organizing a society is according to its labor tasks is also an accurate statement as regards all societies.

9. D: Societal lag is neither a recognized phenomenon of rapid social change, nor a typical reaction to it; the term is a meaningless one. (A) Culture shock, (B) Future shock, (C) Cultural lag, and (E) Patterned evasion are all examples of common reactions by members of a society to rapid social change.

10. B: The fact that numerous airports have not been upgraded to accommodate advances in aviation is an example of cultural lag. (A) Future shock, (C) culture shock, and (D) cultural configuration all describe other types of cultural phenomena which differ from cultural lag. (E) is not an actual phenomenon.

11. A: A sampling method in survey research which relies upon established differences in populations is an example of stratified sampling. (B) Role sampling and (E) correlational sampling are not recognized forms of sampling. (C) Systematic sampling and (D) representative sampling are also wrong answers because they refer to other types of sampling methods which differ from stratified sampling.

12. C: Selection of the individual to be studied is a stage in psychological research which focuses upon the individual, not a stage in sociological research which relies upon the study of a group. (A), (B), (D), and (E) are all recognized steps in sociological research.

13. E: Research methods which focus on personal observations are examples of qualitative methods employed in sociological research. (A), (B), and (C) are incorrect because they all refer to quantitative methods of sociological research. (D) is incorrect because research methods which rely upon studying change are not typical of qualitative methods of sociological research.

14. E: Redundancy is not a part of content analysis; it refers to a mathematical concept unrelated to this type of analysis. (A) Averages (B) means, (C) percentages, and (D) modes are all factors which are considered to be significant in content analysis.

15. D: Issues of individual consent do not provide an ethical dilemma for sociologists because their studies are focused upon groups, not upon individuals. Instead, these issues would provide an ethical dilemma for psychologists because their focus is upon individuals. (A) Invasion of the privacy of the group, (B) method of application of research, and (C) possibility of harm to participants, and (E) the possibility of full disclosure skewing research results are ethical dilemmas for sociologists.

16. A: Sigmund Freud is credited with the founding of psychoanalysis. (B) George Herbert Mead is incorrect because he was involved in social psychology, not psychoanalysis. (C) Charles Horton Cooley is also an incorrect answer because he was a theorist with a background in economics and social psychology. (D) Jean Piaget and (E) Erving Goffman are also incorrect choices because they were, respectively, theorists involved in psychology and sociology.

17. B: The abstract operational phase is not one of Jean Piaget's phases of cognitive development. (A) The sensorimotor phase, (C) the preoperational phase, (D) the concrete operational phase, and (E) the formal operational phase are all, according to Jean Piaget, phases of cognitive development.

18. C: Polyandry is the type of marriage in which one wife is simultaneously married to two or more husbands. (A) Group marriage is incorrect because it describes an arrangement in which several wives are simultaneously married to several husbands. (B) Patrilocality, (D) nuclearity and (E) ritualism are also incorrect choices because they represent concepts unrelated to polyandry.

19. D: According to Max Weber, a characteristic institution reflects the fundamental organization of all societies. (A) A reference group and (B) an in-group are not the right answers because they refer to other phenomena unrelated to a characteristic institution. (C) A bureaucracy is a wrong choice because it reflects the basic organization of some societies, but not of all societies. (E) Nuclear group is not a sociological term; not all societies are organized by nuclear family.

20. C: Screening the subjects is not recognized as a stage of research. (A) Identifying the problem to be studied, (B) finding the appropriate design for research, (D) explaining the final conclusion of the study, and (E) selection and review of pertinent literature are recognized stages of research.

21. B: A post-industrial society's major focus is upon information, rather than upon material goods. (A) A hunting and gathering society, (C) a horticultural society, (D) an agricultural society and (E) an ideological society all have different focuses other than information.

22. D: A status set accurately defines multiple roles of the man described. (A) Ascribed status, (B) master status, (C) achieved status, and (D) salient status all describe single (rather than multiple) roles which a man might assume.

23. B: Deviance does not normally correlate with high intelligence. (A) It offers encouragement that societal controls work, (C) it often correlates with mental illness, (D) it often correlates with criminal behavior, and (E) it often correlates with great ambition are all incorrect choices because they all represent characteristics of deviance.

24. E: The nursing profession is an example of the tertiary sector. (A) The predominant sector, (B) the economic sector, (c) the social sector, and (D) the distributive sector are all incorrect answers because they are not associated with the nursing profession.

25. B: The leaders of a totalitarian government fail to recognize the boundaries of their authority. (A) and (C) are incorrect because there are discernible boundaries as regards the authority of both authoritarian and democratic governments. (D) Systematic and (E) problematic governments are not recognized types of government.

26. A: According to Max Weber, traditional authority (I), rational-legal authority (II), and charismatic authority (III) are the major categories of authority. Democratic authority (IV) is not a category of authority recognized by Weber. (B), (C), (D), and (E) are wrong because they all contain the incorrect answer, democratic authority (IV).

27. B: Theocracy is not a societal function normally associated with religion. It refers, instead, to a type of government. (A), theodicy, (C) codes of ethics, (D) personality, and (E) historical condition are all incorrect because they are societal functions which are usually associated with religion.

28. E: Social status is not a typical source of stratification. (A) Race, (B) age, (C) gender, and (D) sexual preference are all incorrect answers because they do represent typical sources of societal stratification.

29. C: Stereotypes are not among the characteristics usually associated with collective behavior. (A) Fashion, (B) spontaneity, (D) instability, and (E) revolution are all incorrect answers because they represent characteristics normally associated with collective behavior.

30. D: According to C. Wright Mills, the power elite does not include the category of college professors. (A) Business executives, (B) high-ranking military officers, and (C) and (E) government leaders are all incorrect answers because they are all components of C. Wright Mill's power elite.

31. B: Participants in social groups do not tend to display similar qualities. This description refers, instead, to a social category. (A), (C), (D), and (E) are all incorrect answers because they all accurately represent qualities of participants in social groups.

32. A: The major features of a horticultural and pastoral society are the use of hand tools to cultivate plants and the domestication of animals. (B) Agricultural, (C) hunting and gathering, (D) industrial, and (E) postindustrial are all incorrect answers because these societies do not display the major features of cultivating plants and the domestication of animals.

33. D: It is possible to produce big surpluses in an agricultural society. (A), (B), (C), and (D) are all incorrect answers because they all accurately represent characteristics typically found in an agricultural society.

34. D: The type of society whose primary focus is to gather information is an information society, not an industrial one. (A), (B), (C), and (E) are all incorrect answers because they are all characteristics of an industrial society.

35. A: The best characterization of sociocultural evolution is that it describes the inclination of organizations to increase in complexity in the long run. (B) is incorrect because it is the description of society, not of sociocultural evolution. (C) and (D) are also wrong because they describe the ecological approach, not sociocultural evolution. (E) is incorrect because it does not refer to the increasing complexity of cultures.

36. D: The statement that social mobility is unrelated to structural mobility is incorrect. In fact, the opposite is true: social mobility is related to structural mobility. (A), (B), (C), and (D) are incorrect because they do describe characteristics of social mobility.

37. B: Different treatment due to health issues is a concept unrelated to social inequality. (A) Different treatment because of sex, (C) different treatment because of race, (D) different treatment because of age, and (E) different treatment because of religion are all incorrect choices because they are characteristics typical of social inequality.

38. D: is correct because compatibility differences are not among the recognized distinctions often leading to differential treatment in societies. (A) Gender differences, (B) age differences, (C) religious differences, and (E) racial differences are all incorrect answers because they all represent recognized societal distinctions which often lead to differential treatment.

39. E: Although some people from the same social stratum may attempt to be socially mobile, it is incorrect to assume that there is a general tendency among all to aspire towards social mobility. (A), (B), (C), and (D) are incorrect because they each represent characteristics of people from the same social stratum.

40. A: Kingsley Davis (III) and Wilbert Moore (IV) both subscribe to a functionalist view of social stratification. (B), (C), (D), and (E) are incorrect because they include sociologists who do not subscribe to a functionalist view of social stratification (Weber, Marx, and Riesman).

41. B: A grown daughter's living standards improving beyond those of her mother represents absolute mobility. (A) Social hierarchy, (C) relative mobility, (D) social stratification, and (E) social mobility are incorrect selections because they are not examples of this generational improvement in living standards.

42. C: Social hierarchy is an inescapable consequence of social stratification. (A) Social mobility, (B) absolute mobility, (D) social injustice, and (E) social inequality are all incorrect answers because they are not inescapable consequences of social stratification.

43. B: Randall Collins is the sociologist who defines modern conflict theory according to educational credentials. (A) Karl Marx, (C) Ralf Dahrendorf, (D) Max Weber, and (E) Kingsley Davis do not subscribe to this theory.

44. A: During the past 100 years, the most conclusive theories as regards defining unusual collective behavior include the: (I) contagion theory, (IV) convergence theory, and (V) emergent-norm theory. (II) Emergent-image theory and (III) confluence theory are not recognized theories for defining unconventional behavior.

45. A: is the correct answer because it refers to (III), Ralph Turner, and (V), Lewis Killian, who together developed the emergent-norm theory. (B), (C), and (D) are all wrong because none of them include the names of these two founders of the theory. (E) is incorrect because it includes LeBon and King and not Killian.

46. B: is correct because Gustave LeBon is the father of the contagion theory. (A) Lewis Killian, (C) Ralph Turner, (D) Karl Marx, and (E) Ralf Dahrendorf are incorrect answers because they had no involvement in developing this theory.

47. D: If a teenager gives in to the pressures of his high school friends, his behavior is an example of contagion theory. (A) Convergence theory and (B) emergent-norm theory are wrong because they are unrelated to this example. (E) Exchange theory is incorrect because it describes the ways people benefit from each other in social interaction.

48. B: The best definition of convergence theory is that a person is influenced more by his/her own incentives than by those of the group. (A), (C), (D), and (E) are all incorrect because none of them offer definitions of the convergence theory.

49. A: If an adult shoots a thief and others fire their own shots shortly thereafter, this is an illustration of the emergent-norm theory in action. (B), (C), and (D) are incorrect because they are not demonstrations of this theory. (E) is wrong because protesting is not morally ambiguous and booing is not a new norm.

50. C: Riots take more time to complete than mob actions. (A), (B), and (D) are all wrong choices because they are not true statements about riots. (E) Spread of social contagion, which can lead to riots, does not have to be based in fact or verified.

51. C: contains the correct answers: (I) concern about deceiving the individual, and (IV) concern about the risks to the individual. Furthermore, (I) and (IV) are both concerned with the individual; this is actually the focus of psychology rather than of sociology. II, III, and V all pose ethical problems for the sociologist since they are focused upon the group, which is the basis for sociological study.

52. C: The statement that the id provides a system of checks and balances for the ego is not true of Freud's theories in regards to personality. In fact, the opposite is true. Freud believed that the ego provides a system of checks and balances for the id. (A), (B), (D), and (E) are all incorrect answers because each of them represent true statements made by Freud.

53. A: George Herbert Mead did not believe that socialization leads to a facility in identifying deviant behavior. (B), (C), (D), and (E) all accurately refer to Mead's theories.

54. E: The dramaturgical approach involves "impression management", which hopes to influence how a person is perceived by others. Controlling the way others perceive a person is not possible. (A), (B), and (C) represent different facets of Goffman's beliefs about the self. (D), which describes the differences between the authentic self and the public portrayal of self, is Goffman's definition of role-distance.

55. B: Charles Horton Cooley did not espouse the theory that the self-concept is fragile and easily damaged. (A), (C), (D), and (E) are all among Cooley's theories.

56. E: is the correct answer because the rebellious teenage phase is not one of Erikson's phases of ego formation. (A), (B), (C), and (D) are all incorrect answers in that they each accurately represent a particular phase of ego formation as described by Erikson.

57. E: Kohlberg theorized that moral thinking developed as people grew older, not that it was constant throughout life. (A) Kohlberg believed that moral reasoning evolves through six basic steps, (B) he was strongly influenced by Jean Piaget, (C) many have considered him to have been short-sighted in regard to women, and (D) he believed that adolescence was a key step in the development of morals.

58. E: According to Carol Gilligan, (A) women tend to approach ethical challenges from the perspective of responsibility, (B) men tend to approach ethical challenges from the perspective of ultimate results, (C) boys and girls present fundamental differences as to how their psyches operate, and (D) the two sexes approach problem-solving differently because of their divergent social roles. (E) is not part of Carol Gilligan's viewpoint.

59. A: Polygyny is the societal custom in which a husband simultaneously has two or more wives. (B) Kinship, (C) group marriage, and (D) patrilocality do not describe this type of societal custom. (E) Mormonism is incorrect because it describes a specific religion, not a type of societal custom.

60. E: A significant result of deviance is not that it often destroys a group. (A), A social group can frequently become united as a result of deviance, (B), clear boundaries of appropriate behavior are delineated by deviance, (C), a reasonable method of protest is provided through deviance, and (D), both formal and informal controls over society are provided by deviance, are all incorrect answers because they are true of deviance.

61. B: Group marriage is a type of marriage in which multiple women are simultaneously married to multiple men. (A) Monogamy is incorrect because it defines a marriage between one man and one woman only. (C) Mormonism is wrong because it describes a religion, not a type of marriage. (D) Mutual consent is an incorrect answer because it is not a recognized form of marriage. (E) Polygyny, which refers to the societal custom in which the husband simultaneously has two or more wives, is also wrong because it refers to a different type of marriage.

62. C: The fact that Americans forbid marriage between immediate family members is an example of exogamy. (A) Monogamy and (B) polygamy are incorrect because they refer to certain types of marriage which differ from exogamy. (D) Kinship and (E) nuclearity are wrong answers because they are concepts which are not associated with exogamy.

63. A: If the authority of the family rests with the mother, this is an example of a matriarchy. (B) Matrilocality is incorrect because it describes the custom of newlyweds living under the same roof as the wife's extended family. (C) Matrilineal society is wrong because it refers to the procedure of tracing a family's lineage through the mother. (D) Matrimonial society is incorrect because it is not a recognized type of society. (E) Matricentricity does not describe patterns of authority.

64. E: Patriarchy describes a system in which family systems are organized around father-rule and male authority. (A), which states that a patriarchy can be matrilineal, and (B), which states that a patriarchy can be matrilocal, are both incorrect answers because they are, in fact, characteristics of patriarchies. (C), which states that the levirate is sometimes present in this society, and (D), which states that primogeniture is sometimes present in this society, are also incorrect choices because they are possible traits of a patriarchy as well.

65. D: A patriarchal society is one in which the family's authority rests with the father. (A) Patrimonial is incorrect because it describes a different type of society which is based upon its ancestors. (B) Patrilineal is a wrong choice because it refers to a method of tracing family lineage, not to a type of society. (C) Patronizing is incorrect because it is not a recognized type of society. (E) Paternal is an incorrect answer because it refers to anything associated with fatherhood, and because it is also not a recognized type of society.

66. A: Endogamy is the societal custom of only allowing marriage between individuals belonging to the same, or similar, groups. (B) Nuclearity is wrong because it is not a recognized societal custom. (C) Integration is an incorrect answer because it represents a social concept different from endogamy. (D) Monogamy and (E) polyandry are both wrong because they refer to marital arrangements which differ from endogamy.

67. B: Serial monogamy describes a situation in which a person marries once, later divorces, and then marries once again. (A) Polygamy is incorrect because it describes the societal custom of having more than one spouse at a time. (C) Deviance is a social concept unrelated to serial monogamy and is, therefore, a wrong answer. (D) Matrimony is incorrect because it is merely another word for marriage. (E) is incorrect because stigma is not associated with serial monogamy.

68. A: If a father from a patriarchal society passes on his property to his youngest son, he is practicing ultimogeniture. (B) Primogeniture is incorrect because it refers to the practice of a father's passing his property to his eldest son, not his youngest. (C) Neolocality and (D) patrilocality are incorrect because they represent concepts unrelated to ultimogeniture. (E) Parsimony is incorrect because is it not a societal practice; it is merely another word for stinginess.

69. C: A pattern of tracing family lineage through the mother's side of the family is an example of matrilineal research. (A) Matrilocal is incorrect because it describes the custom in which newlyweds live under the same roof with the wife's extended family. (B) Matriarchal is wrong because it refers to a society in which the mother holds the authority. (D) Matrimonial is incorrect because it refers to anything associated with marriage, not specifically to the practice of tracing family lineage. (E) Maternal is also not the correct answer because it is a general term used to describe anything about mothers and is not a type of family research.

70. E: Sutherland studied white-collar crime in contrast to his predecessors who thought that criminal behavior was found more prevalently in people in the lower class. According to Southerland, (A) primary groups are the breeding ground for criminal behavior, (B) social interaction can teach criminal behavior, (C) childhood is often the time when people learn to be criminals, and (D) criminal behavior is tied to a belief in its advantages are all beliefs which are fundamental to Sutherland's theories of criminal behavior.

71. B: The teaching profession today is an example of relative mobility. (A) Relative stratification, (C) relative orientation, (D) relative structure, and (E) relative status are all incorrect because they are not recognized patterns of social stratification.

72. E: Social bonds is the only phrase that does not pertain to social stratification, or social layering in accordance with power, wealth, or honor. This can happen according to race and ethnicity, gender, age, and sexual preference, among other things. Marx's false consciousness, status attainment theory, visibility and markers, and India's caste system are all related to social stratification.

73. D: Modern conflict theory does not place an emphasis upon an individual's self-awareness. (A), (B), (C), and (E) each accurately describe interpretations of the bases of modern conflict theory.

74. C: A cult is a group which has a charismatic leader, voluntary membership, and reflects the most basic type of organizational structure possible. (A), Church, and (B), sect, may or may not have charismatic leaders, voluntary membership and the most basic type of organizational structure, making these choices incorrect. (D) Fad is incorrect because it doesn't have a leader or membership and (E) is wrong because, among other things, it is not the most basic type of organizational structure.

75. B: A church's membership is not based upon social stratification. (A), (C), (D), and (E) all describe traits regularly associated with the definition of a church.

76. A: Faiths based in East Asia and parts of Southeast Asia do not emphasize the teaching and learning of religious doctrines. (B), (C), (D), and (E) do, in fact, represent traits present in the faiths of Southeast Asia and East Asia.

77. D: The statement that collective behavior rarely changes is false. In fact, the opposite is true; it changes a great deal. (A), (B), (C), and (E) are all incorrect answers because they are all characteristics of collective behavior.

78. D: is the correct answer because the most accurate definition of propaganda is that it entails efforts to alter public opinion. (A), (B), and (C) are incorrect answers because they are not definitions of propaganda. (E) is wrong because propaganda is not just political.

79. D: I and III only is the correct answer because there are no major studies of social problems resulting from social stratification worldwide in the areas of (I) domestic abuse or (III) date rape.

80. C: Social stratification is not affected by (I) manual, (II) domestic, (III) environmental, and/or (IV) national dimensions. A, B, and E are all incorrect because they all contain the wrong answer, (V). (D) is wrong because it fails to mention the additional correct answers (I), (III), and (IV).

81. E: Race (IV) is not one of Max Weber's independent factors which form the basis for his theory of stratification. (I), (II), and (III) are all incorrect because they are among Weber's independent factors forming his theory of stratification.

82. A: The middle class is not one of Max Weber's major classes of society. (B) The most affluent class (upper class), (C) the petite bourgeoisie, (D) the class of manual laborers, and (E) white-collar workers are Max Weber's major societal classes.

83. A: If a supervisor who needs to be firm with employees as regards output and deadlines also likes to go bowling with them on the weekends, this is an example of role strain. (B) Role conflict,

(C) role play, (D) role reversal, and (E) role distance are all incorrect answers because they do not describe the given situation.

84. C: The description of Susan as a licensed psychologist, a status which she has personally attained, is a description of her achieved status. (A) Ascribed status is incorrect because it refers to a different type of status which is assigned to an individual and has nothing to do with one's own personal achievements. (B) Inferred status and (E) adopted status are not recognized types of status. (D) Master status is incorrect because it represents a more comprehensive definition of someone's status than does achieved status.

85. A: According to Ferdinand Tonnies, a good definition of gemeinschaft is community. (B) Society, (C) dyad, (D) triad, and (E) role play are all wrong because they are not definitions of gemeinschaft.

86. D: Conglomerates is the correct answer because this is not a major category of groups which sociologists have traditionally studied. (A) Aggregates, (B) families, (C) peer groups, and (E) secondary groups are all incorrect answers because they all represent important categories of groups which sociologists have traditionally studied.

87. B: If a sociologist were to blindly choose the necessary number of cards with names on them for potential research subjects, she is putting together a random sample. (A) Representative sample, (C) systematic sample, and (D) stratified sample are incorrect answers because they represent different types of samples than do random samples. (E) Descriptive sample is wrong because it is not a recognized type of sample.

88. E: When Elton May found in his studies that the sociologist's presence during research can alter the behavior of the participants, he actually discovered the Hawthorne effect. (A) Control group effect, (B) content analysis effect, (C) random sample effect, and (D) stratification effect are not recognized influences upon the research subject's behavior.

89. A: Talcott Parsons is the sociologist credited with discovering the grand theory of society. (B) Robert Merton, (C) C. Wright Mills, (D) Dennis Wong, and (E) Erving Goffman are all incorrect answers because they are not founders of this theory.

90. E: Stratification is the correct answer because it is not a type of religious group. (A) Cult, (B) sect, (C) church, and (D) temple are all incorrect answers because they all represent various types of religious groups.

91. E: Manufacturing cars is the correct answer because it is not associated with the primary sector of the economy. It is, instead, associated with its secondary sector. (A) Hunting deer, (B) gathering plants and herbs, (C) panning for gold, and (D) farming are all incorrect answers because they are all associated with the primary economic sector.

92. B: Manufacturing weapons is the correct answer because it is associated with the secondary sector of the economy. (A) Panning for gold is incorrect because it is an activity associated with the primary economic sector, not with the secondary one. (C) Providing electrical wiring, (D) providing physical therapy, and (E) teaching Spanish are all wrong answers because they are associated with the tertiary economic sector, not the secondary one.

93. A: As an occupational therapist, Robert works in the service sector. (B) Manufacturing is incorrect because it is a profession associated with the secondary economic sector. (C) Production, (D) cultivation, and (E) free market are all wrong answers because they are not recognized economic sectors.

94. C: Mining diamonds is a profession associated with the primary economic sector. (A) Knitting, (D) mending clothes, and (E) repairing jewelry are all incorrect answers because they are professions associated with the tertiary sector, not with the primary economic sector. (B) Making rugs is also a wrong answer because it is a profession associated with the secondary economic sector.

95. C: The production and profitable sale of a variety of both goods and services includes the service sector (V) only. (A), (B), (D), and (E) are all incorrect answers because they each include one or more incorrect choices.

96. A: Economic distribution systems encompass all of the systems mentioned except the secondary sector. (B) The free market system, (C) the barter system, (D) the direct exchange, which is another way of describing the barter system, and (E) the informal sector each represent a type of economic distribution system.

97. D: Every individual in a multi-racial society undergoes a degree of racial or ethnic socialization. The statements in (A), (B), (C), and (E) all describe racial socialization.

98. A: The statement that ethnicity sometimes refers to the ability of a group to move through the social strata is incorrect. This definition is actually of social mobility, not of ethnicity. (B) It sometimes refers to a group recognized by its shared language, (C) it sometimes refers to a group which shares a national heritage, (D) it is sometimes used as a means of enacting social stratification, and (E) it is sometimes based upon differences taught and learned in the particular culture are all incorrect answers because they are descriptive of ethnicity.

99. E: Traits associated with gender differences include all but differences in ethnic roles. (A) Differences in hairstyles, (B) differences in clothing, (C) differences in family position, and (D) differences in professions are all incorrect answers because they all represent traits associated with gender differences.

100. B: This treatment of Bill is an example of age stratification. (A) Age conflict theory, (C) age exception, (D) age orientation, and (E) age functionalism are not recognized theories in sociology.

How to Overcome Test Anxiety

Just the thought of taking a test is enough to make most people a little nervous. A test is an important event that can have a long-term impact on your future, so it's important to take it seriously and it's natural to feel anxious about performing well. But just because anxiety is normal, that doesn't mean that it's helpful in test taking, or that you should simply accept it as part of your life. Anxiety can have a variety of effects. These effects can be mild, like making you feel slightly nervous, or severe, like blocking your ability to focus or remember even a simple detail.

If you experience test anxiety—whether severe or mild—it's important to know how to beat it. To discover this, first you need to understand what causes test anxiety.

Causes of Test Anxiety

While we often think of anxiety as an uncontrollable emotional state, it can actually be caused by simple, practical things. One of the most common causes of test anxiety is that a person does not feel adequately prepared for their test. This feeling can be the result of many different issues such as poor study habits or lack of organization, but the most common culprit is time management. Starting to study too late, failing to organize your study time to cover all of the material, or being distracted while you study will mean that you're not well prepared for the test. This may lead to cramming the night before, which will cause you to be physically and mentally exhausted for the test. Poor time management also contributes to feelings of stress, fear, and hopelessness as you realize you are not well prepared but don't know what to do about it.

Other times, test anxiety is not related to your preparation for the test but comes from unresolved fear. This may be a past failure on a test, or poor performance on tests in general. It may come from comparing yourself to others who seem to be performing better or from the stress of living up to expectations. Anxiety may be driven by fears of the future—how failure on this test would affect your educational and career goals. These fears are often completely irrational, but they can still negatively impact your test performance.

> **Review Video:** <u>3 Reasons You Have Test Anxiety</u>
> Visit mometrix.com/academy and enter code: 428468

Elements of Test Anxiety

As mentioned earlier, test anxiety is considered to be an emotional state, but it has physical and mental components as well. Sometimes you may not even realize that you are suffering from test anxiety until you notice the physical symptoms. These can include trembling hands, rapid heartbeat, sweating, nausea, and tense muscles. Extreme anxiety may lead to fainting or vomiting. Obviously, any of these symptoms can have a negative impact on testing. It is important to recognize them as soon as they begin to occur so that you can address the problem before it damages your performance.

> **Review Video: 3 Ways to Tell You Have Test Anxiety**
> Visit mometrix.com/academy and enter code: 927847

The mental components of test anxiety include trouble focusing and inability to remember learned information. During a test, your mind is on high alert, which can help you recall information and stay focused for an extended period of time. However, anxiety interferes with your mind's natural processes, causing you to blank out, even on the questions you know well. The strain of testing during anxiety makes it difficult to stay focused, especially on a test that may take several hours. Extreme anxiety can take a huge mental toll, making it difficult not only to recall test information but even to understand the test questions or pull your thoughts together.

> **Review Video: How Test Anxiety Affects Memory**
> Visit mometrix.com/academy and enter code: 609003

Effects of Test Anxiety

Test anxiety is like a disease—if left untreated, it will get progressively worse. Anxiety leads to poor performance, and this reinforces the feelings of fear and failure, which in turn lead to poor performances on subsequent tests. It can grow from a mild nervousness to a crippling condition. If allowed to progress, test anxiety can have a big impact on your schooling, and consequently on your future.

Test anxiety can spread to other parts of your life. Anxiety on tests can become anxiety in any stressful situation, and blanking on a test can turn into panicking in a job situation. But fortunately, you don't have to let anxiety rule your testing and determine your grades. There are a number of relatively simple steps you can take to move past anxiety and function normally on a test and in the rest of life.

> **Review Video: How Test Anxiety Impacts Your Grades**
> Visit mometrix.com/academy and enter code: 939819

Physical Steps for Beating Test Anxiety

While test anxiety is a serious problem, the good news is that it can be overcome. It doesn't have to control your ability to think and remember information. While it may take time, you can begin taking steps today to beat anxiety.

Just as your first hint that you may be struggling with anxiety comes from the physical symptoms, the first step to treating it is also physical. Rest is crucial for having a clear, strong mind. If you are tired, it is much easier to give in to anxiety. But if you establish good sleep habits, your body and mind will be ready to perform optimally, without the strain of exhaustion. Additionally, sleeping well helps you to retain information better, so you're more likely to recall the answers when you see the test questions.

Getting good sleep means more than going to bed on time. It's important to allow your brain time to relax. Take study breaks from time to time so it doesn't get overworked, and don't study right before bed. Take time to rest your mind before trying to rest your body, or you may find it difficult to fall asleep.

> **Review Video:** **The Importance of Sleep for Your Brain**
> Visit mometrix.com/academy and enter code: 319338

Along with sleep, other aspects of physical health are important in preparing for a test. Good nutrition is vital for good brain function. Sugary foods and drinks may give a burst of energy but this burst is followed by a crash, both physically and emotionally. Instead, fuel your body with protein and vitamin-rich foods.

Also, drink plenty of water. Dehydration can lead to headaches and exhaustion, especially if your brain is already under stress from the rigors of the test. Particularly if your test is a long one, drink water during the breaks. And if possible, take an energy-boosting snack to eat between sections.

> **Review Video:** **How Diet Can Affect your Mood**
> Visit mometrix.com/academy and enter code: 624317

Along with sleep and diet, a third important part of physical health is exercise. Maintaining a steady workout schedule is helpful, but even taking 5-minute study breaks to walk can help get your blood pumping faster and clear your head. Exercise also releases endorphins, which contribute to a positive feeling and can help combat test anxiety.

When you nurture your physical health, you are also contributing to your mental health. If your body is healthy, your mind is much more likely to be healthy as well. So take time to rest, nourish your body with healthy food and water, and get moving as much as possible. Taking these physical steps will make you stronger and more able to take the mental steps necessary to overcome test anxiety.

Mental Steps for Beating Test Anxiety

Working on the mental side of test anxiety can be more challenging, but as with the physical side, there are clear steps you can take to overcome it. As mentioned earlier, test anxiety often stems from lack of preparation, so the obvious solution is to prepare for the test. Effective studying may be the most important weapon you have for beating test anxiety, but you can and should employ several other mental tools to combat fear.

First, boost your confidence by reminding yourself of past success—tests or projects that you aced. If you're putting as much effort into preparing for this test as you did for those, there's no reason you should expect to fail here. Work hard to prepare; then trust your preparation.

Second, surround yourself with encouraging people. It can be helpful to find a study group, but be sure that the people you're around will encourage a positive attitude. If you spend time with others who are anxious or cynical, this will only contribute to your own anxiety. Look for others who are motivated to study hard from a desire to succeed, not from a fear of failure.

Third, reward yourself. A test is physically and mentally tiring, even without anxiety, and it can be helpful to have something to look forward to. Plan an activity following the test, regardless of the outcome, such as going to a movie or getting ice cream.

When you are taking the test, if you find yourself beginning to feel anxious, remind yourself that you know the material. Visualize successfully completing the test. Then take a few deep, relaxing breaths and return to it. Work through the questions carefully but with confidence, knowing that you are capable of succeeding.

Developing a healthy mental approach to test taking will also aid in other areas of life. Test anxiety affects more than just the actual test—it can be damaging to your mental health and even contribute to depression. It's important to beat test anxiety before it becomes a problem for more than testing.

Review Video: <u>Test Anxiety and Depression</u>
Visit mometrix.com/academy and enter code: 904704

Study Strategy

Being prepared for the test is necessary to combat anxiety, but what does being prepared look like? You may study for hours on end and still not feel prepared. What you need is a strategy for test prep. The next few pages outline our recommended steps to help you plan out and conquer the challenge of preparation.

Step 1: Scope Out the Test

Learn everything you can about the format (multiple choice, essay, etc.) and what will be on the test. Gather any study materials, course outlines, or sample exams that may be available. Not only will this help you to prepare, but knowing what to expect can help to alleviate test anxiety.

Step 2: Map Out the Material

Look through the textbook or study guide and make note of how many chapters or sections it has. Then divide these over the time you have. For example, if a book has 15 chapters and you have five days to study, you need to cover three chapters each day. Even better, if you have the time, leave an extra day at the end for overall review after you have gone through the material in depth.

If time is limited, you may need to prioritize the material. Look through it and make note of which sections you think you already have a good grasp on, and which need review. While you are studying, skim quickly through the familiar sections and take more time on the challenging parts. Write out your plan so you don't get lost as you go. Having a written plan also helps you feel more in control of the study, so anxiety is less likely to arise from feeling overwhelmed at the amount to cover.

Step 3: Gather Your Tools

Decide what study method works best for you. Do you prefer to highlight in the book as you study and then go back over the highlighted portions? Or do you type out notes of the important information? Or is it helpful to make flashcards that you can carry with you? Assemble the pens, index cards, highlighters, post-it notes, and any other materials you may need so you won't be distracted by getting up to find things while you study.

If you're having a hard time retaining the information or organizing your notes, experiment with different methods. For example, try color-coding by subject with colored pens, highlighters, or post-it notes. If you learn better by hearing, try recording yourself reading your notes so you can listen while in the car, working out, or simply sitting at your desk. Ask a friend to quiz you from your flashcards, or try teaching someone the material to solidify it in your mind.

Step 4: Create Your Environment

It's important to avoid distractions while you study. This includes both the obvious distractions like visitors and the subtle distractions like an uncomfortable chair (or a too-comfortable couch that makes you want to fall asleep). Set up the best study environment possible: good lighting and a comfortable work area. If background music helps you focus, you may want to turn it on, but otherwise keep the room quiet. If you are using a computer to take notes, be sure you don't have any other windows open, especially applications like social media, games, or anything else that could distract you. Silence your phone and turn off notifications. Be sure to keep water close by so you stay hydrated while you study (but avoid unhealthy drinks and snacks).

Also, take into account the best time of day to study. Are you freshest first thing in the morning? Try to set aside some time then to work through the material. Is your mind clearer in the afternoon or evening? Schedule your study session then. Another method is to study at the same time of day that you will take the test, so that your brain gets used to working on the material at that time and will be ready to focus at test time.

Step 5: Study!

Once you have done all the study preparation, it's time to settle into the actual studying. Sit down, take a few moments to settle your mind so you can focus, and begin to follow your study plan. Don't give in to distractions or let yourself procrastinate. This is your time to prepare so you'll be ready to fearlessly approach the test. Make the most of the time and stay focused.

Of course, you don't want to burn out. If you study too long you may find that you're not retaining the information very well. Take regular study breaks. For example, taking five minutes out of every hour to walk briskly, breathing deeply and swinging your arms, can help your mind stay fresh.

As you get to the end of each chapter or section, it's a good idea to do a quick review. Remind yourself of what you learned and work on any difficult parts. When you feel that you've mastered the material, move on to the next part. At the end of your study session, briefly skim through your notes again.

But while review is helpful, cramming last minute is NOT. If at all possible, work ahead so that you won't need to fit all your study into the last day. Cramming overloads your brain with more information than it can process and retain, and your tired mind may struggle to recall even previously learned information when it is overwhelmed with last-minute study. Also, the urgent nature of cramming and the stress placed on your brain contribute to anxiety. You'll be more likely to go to the test feeling unprepared and having trouble thinking clearly.

So don't cram, and don't stay up late before the test, even just to review your notes at a leisurely pace. Your brain needs rest more than it needs to go over the information again. In fact, plan to finish your studies by noon or early afternoon the day before the test. Give your brain the rest of the day to relax or focus on other things, and get a good night's sleep. Then you will be fresh for the test and better able to recall what you've studied.

Step 6: Take a practice test

Many courses offer sample tests, either online or in the study materials. This is an excellent resource to check whether you have mastered the material, as well as to prepare for the test format and environment.

Check the test format ahead of time: the number of questions, the type (multiple choice, free response, etc.), and the time limit. Then create a plan for working through them. For example, if you have 30 minutes to take a 60-question test, your limit is 30 seconds per question. Spend less time on the questions you know well so that you can take more time on the difficult ones.

If you have time to take several practice tests, take the first one open book, with no time limit. Work through the questions at your own pace and make sure you fully understand them. Gradually work up to taking a test under test conditions: sit at a desk with all study materials put away and set a timer. Pace yourself to make sure you finish the test with time to spare and go back to check your answers if you have time.

After each test, check your answers. On the questions you missed, be sure you understand why you missed them. Did you misread the question (tests can use tricky wording)? Did you forget the information? Or was it something you hadn't learned? Go back and study any shaky areas that the practice tests reveal.

Taking these tests not only helps with your grade, but also aids in combating test anxiety. If you're already used to the test conditions, you're less likely to worry about it, and working through tests until you're scoring well gives you a confidence boost. Go through the practice tests until you feel comfortable, and then you can go into the test knowing that you're ready for it.

Test Tips

On test day, you should be confident, knowing that you've prepared well and are ready to answer the questions. But aside from preparation, there are several test day strategies you can employ to maximize your performance.

First, as stated before, get a good night's sleep the night before the test (and for several nights before that, if possible). Go into the test with a fresh, alert mind rather than staying up late to study.

Try not to change too much about your normal routine on the day of the test. It's important to eat a nutritious breakfast, but if you normally don't eat breakfast at all, consider eating just a protein bar. If you're a coffee drinker, go ahead and have your normal coffee. Just make sure you time it so that the caffeine doesn't wear off right in the middle of your test. Avoid sugary beverages, and drink enough water to stay hydrated but not so much that you need a restroom break 10 minutes into the test. If your test isn't first thing in the morning, consider going for a walk or doing a light workout before the test to get your blood flowing.

Allow yourself enough time to get ready, and leave for the test with plenty of time to spare so you won't have the anxiety of scrambling to arrive in time. Another reason to be early is to select a good seat. It's helpful to sit away from doors and windows, which can be distracting. Find a good seat, get out your supplies, and settle your mind before the test begins.

When the test begins, start by going over the instructions carefully, even if you already know what to expect. Make sure you avoid any careless mistakes by following the directions.

Then begin working through the questions, pacing yourself as you've practiced. If you're not sure on an answer, don't spend too much time on it, and don't let it shake your confidence. Either skip it and come back later, or eliminate as many wrong answers as possible and guess among the remaining ones. Don't dwell on these questions as you continue—put them out of your mind and focus on what lies ahead.

Be sure to read all of the answer choices, even if you're sure the first one is the right answer. Sometimes you'll find a better one if you keep reading. But don't second-guess yourself if you do immediately know the answer. Your gut instinct is usually right. Don't let test anxiety rob you of the information you know.

If you have time at the end of the test (and if the test format allows), go back and review your answers. Be cautious about changing any, since your first instinct tends to be correct, but make sure you didn't misread any of the questions or accidentally mark the wrong answer choice. Look over any you skipped and make an educated guess.

At the end, leave the test feeling confident. You've done your best, so don't waste time worrying about your performance or wishing you could change anything. Instead, celebrate the successful completion of this test. And finally, use this test to learn how to deal with anxiety even better next time.

Review Video: 5 Tips to Beat Test Anxiety
Visit mometrix.com/academy and enter code: 570656

Important Qualification

Not all anxiety is created equal. If your test anxiety is causing major issues in your life beyond the classroom or testing center, or if you are experiencing troubling physical symptoms related to your anxiety, it may be a sign of a serious physiological or psychological condition. If this sounds like your situation, we strongly encourage you to seek professional help.

Thank You

We at Mometrix would like to extend our heartfelt thanks to you, our friend and patron, for allowing us to play a part in your journey. It is a privilege to serve people from all walks of life who are unified in their commitment to building the best future they can for themselves.

The preparation you devote to these important testing milestones may be the most valuable educational opportunity you have for making a real difference in your life. We encourage you to put your heart into it—that feeling of succeeding, overcoming, and yes, conquering will be well worth the hours you've invested.

We want to hear your story, your struggles and your successes, and if you see any opportunities for us to improve our materials so we can help others even more effectively in the future, please share that with us as well. **The team at Mometrix would be absolutely thrilled to hear from you!** So please, send us an email (support@mometrix.com) and let's stay in touch.

If you'd like some additional help, check out these other resources we offer for your exam:

http://MometrixFlashcards.com/CLEP

Additional Bonus Material

Due to our efforts to try to keep this book to a manageable length, we've created a link that will give you access to all of your additional bonus material.

Please visit http://www.mometrix.com/bonus948/clepintrosocio to access the information.